# LOVING YOUR PLACE ON THE SPECTRUM

A Neurodiversity Blueprint

# LOVING YOUR PLACE ON THE SPECTRUM

# JUDE MORROW

Foreword by Tim Goldstein

BEYOND WORDS
Portland, Oregon

**BEYOND** WORDS

1750 S.W. Skyline Blvd, Suite 20
Portland, Oregon 97221-2543
503-531-8700 / 503-531-8773 fax
www.beyondword.com

First Beyond Words paperback edition September 2021

The information contained in this book is intended to be educational and not for diagnosis, prescription, or treatment of any health disorder whatsoever. It is intended to provide helpful and informative material on the subjects addressed in the publication. It is sold with the understanding that the author and publisher are not engaged in rendering medical, health, or any other kind of personal professional services in the book. The reader should consult his or her medical, health, or other competent professional before adopting any of the suggestions in this book or drawing inferences from it. The author and publisher specifically disclaim all responsibility for any liability, loss, or risk, personal or otherwise, which is incurred as a consequence, directly or indirectly, of the use and application of any of the contents of this book.

**BEYOND WORDS** PUBLISHING and colophon are registered trademarks of Beyond Words Publishing. Beyond Words is an imprint of Simon & Schuster, Inc.

For more information about special discounts for bulk purchases, please contact Beyond Words Special Sales at 503-531-8700 or specialsales@beyondword.com.

Managing editor: Lindsay S. Easterbrooks-Brown
Editor: Brit Elders
Copyeditor: Ashley Van Winkle
Proofreader: Olivia Rollins
Design: Devon Smith
Composition: William H. Brunson Typography Services

Manufactured in the United States of America

10 9 8 7 6 5 4 3 2 1

Library of Congress Cataloging-in-Publication Data:

Names: Morrow, Jude, 1990- author.
Title: Loving your place on the spectrum : a neurodiversity blueprint /
   Jude Morrow ; foreword by Tim Goldstein.
Description: First Beyond Words hardcover edition. | Portland, Oregon :
   Beyond Words, 2021. | Includes bibliographical references.
Identifiers: LCCN 2021011054 (print) | LCCN 2021011055 (ebook) |
ISBN 9781582708331 (trade paperback) | ISBN 9781582708386 (ebook)
Subjects: LCSH: Asperger's syndrome—Patients. | Autism spectrum
   disorders—Patients. | Autistic people—Family.
Classification: LCC RC553.A88 M6789 2021 (print) | LCC RC553.A88 (ebook)
   | DDC 616.85/8832—dc23
LC record available at https://lccn.loc.gov/2021011054
LC ebook record available at https://lccn.loc.gov/2021011055

The corporate mission of Beyond Words Publishing, Inc.: *Inspire to Integrity*

For all autistic and neurodiverse people, young and old.

# Contents

# Foreword

## by Tim Goldstein

I met Jude on LinkedIn, where I frequently meet fascinating autistic professionals of all backgrounds, industries, races, genders, and countries. Jude did something many think autistic folks are incapable of and most people connect with them, miss. He introduced himself with a very short yet professional overview of himself and his book. He made a specific request: "Would you help me to spread the word?" I read his book and we had a long video chat. I found a new friend who gets it!

Jude's work immerses him in a world where being autistic is frequently seen as something to fix. With the experience of building a successful autistic adult life, he knows the truth is quite different. Jude writes in a clear and humorous style which recognizes all humans fit in the Neuro Cloud™ with its full range and mixture of all possible human traits.

The world is slowly waking up to the fact that autism is not just young boys. In the adult autistic community and moving into the rest of the world is a uniting movement: neurodiversity. Instead of looking at the majority of humans as "normal" and those who perceive, process, or think differently as broken "normal" people who need to be fixed, I see it through the neurodiverse, humanity-encompassing Neuro Cloud™ concept. This model of neurodiversity aligns with general diversity by acknowledging it takes all humans to express the full range of diversity and all ways of thinking for the full range of human neurodiversity.

Neurodiversity is the idea that our brains vary greatly in how they are shaped, how they are wired, and how they function. Further, we believe these differences cause a range of perception, processing, and thinking methods. The Neuro Cloud™ concept arranges the building blocks of neurodiversity, presented by Judy Singer in her thesis paper, so they parallel diversity in the way the words and thoughts mix. There has not been a universal definition of neurodiversity or the words used to describe it. People are left unclear whether a non-neurotypical is neuro-distinct, neurodiverse, or neurodivergent. It leaves many confused and others clinging to wording which doesn't logically make sense.

The Neuro Cloud™ starts with the belief that neurodiversity includes every way humans can think or be. No one lives outside the cloud. Aligning with diversity helps many understand neurodiversity by putting it in a context more widely known. Diversity talks about the makeup of a group as being diverse or not. In the Neuro Cloud™, neurodiverse is not a name for a sub-population, but like diversity, a relative representation regarding the makeup of a group. When I say a group is neurodiverse, I am telling you it has a representative mix of perceiving and thinking styles, just as saying the group is diverse means a representation of all diversity. It does not indicate specific styles, just inclusion of a wide range of styles.

If neurodiversity means everyone, how do we refer to general groupings which see the world in different ways? Humans have a historical pattern where a large segment perceives and thinks in similar ways. This creates a dominant group that most consider "normal." In neurodiversity, just as with diversity, this majority group believes their ways are right because their vast numbers make them common. While they are not defined by any special characteristic besides their numbers, we refer to them as neurotypical. There is nothing special about being neurotypical other than you are a member of the largest area of the Neuro Cloud™.

The overwhelming size of the neurotypical community has allowed them to set the norms we live by and makes them predominate. With neurotypical being just one of many ways for humans to be, in the Neuro Cloud™ we refer to people who are not neurotypical as neurodistinct. Neurodistinct is easy to understand: someone who perceives, processes, or thinks in a distinctly different manner than neurotypicals. Not being neurotypical no longer means you are divergent, which seems like a negative curse word to me, but that you have distinctly different, alternate ways which may be improvements on the neurotypical norms.

Where does the cloud portion of the Neuro Cloud™ fit in besides that there are two main groups? Neurotypical is the majority and neurodistinct is the minority. In the Neuro Cloud™ we view all traits as human traits in varying levels. The cloud fits by illustrating how there are no distinct partitions or boundaries within it, but instead an ever-moving and ever-mixing set of traits and thinking. Through viewing all traits as human traits, we quickly recognize that the bundle of traits we associate with various mental and cognitive distinctions are not only arbitrary but frequently present in many without the particular "condition."

I fall into the better-known geek/techie motif of autism and lack many of Jude's abilities to interact with people at a level to have a career as a social worker. This difference between us is a great example of neurodistinct individuals demonstrating drastically different levels of human traits. While both Jude and I are autistic and do have common interests, we are very different in our interactional strengths and weaknesses. Further proof the Neuro Cloud™ is a much better view than the rigid medical model which sees us both as autistic and needing to be fixed instead of seeing us as individual humans with innovative thoughts and ways to be.

Jude created an amazing resource with this book. He covers some of the most challenging aspects of life for a neurodistinct autistic individual from the neurodistinct perspective but expressed in terms that the entire neurodiverse universe can understand. He exposes the fictional stereotypes that are so damaging to neurodistinct people. An autistic person isn't this way or that way any more than any individual from any group is any certain way. The main point that both Jude, through his book, and I, through the Neuro Cloud™, want the world to understand is we are just as normal as any human. While some of us need tools and techniques to better interact with the rest of the Neuro Cloud™, that doesn't mean we need to be fixed. Instead, we *all* need to be trained to build a bridge of understanding and acceptance, neurotypical or neurodistinct.

# Preface

S ince accepting and coming to terms with the fact that I am autistic, my life has become a vast ocean of opportunities and love. Being different was never easy and, as a child, I always believed my life consisted of obstacles blocking my path, overcoming one and then waiting for another obstacle to come along sooner or later. For my past and future, I learned to change the lens through which I view both. Instead of focusing on the obstacles that were in my path, I focused on overcoming. With that mind-set, I now view my life as one victory after another! I managed to do this without changing the narrative of my journey from autistic child to autistic man. With the pages ahead, you can too.

Following the release of my first book, *Why Does Daddy Always Look So Sad?*, I hit the road. I traveled the length and breadth of Ireland meeting parental support groups, schools, and other autistic people like me. During my maiden speaking tour, I told my story in the hope that it would inspire parents and autistic children to know that we can grow to live happy and successful lives. When meeting with medical and educational professionals, I challenged the myths surrounding autism and certainly opened some perspectives along the way. I never in my wildest dreams thought my story would be one of interest, intrigue, and inquisitiveness.

I do not stand on the stage as an expert, just an autistic man who wants to extend his hand and tell his story to those who are willing to open their ears and hearts to hear it. During this process, I had to open my own ears and heart too! Fellow autistic people educated me about the struggles faced today and how we can overcome them as a global family. I realized how little I knew about the autistic community that I was part of.

I learned of the neurodiversity movement and how it aims to change and eradicate outdated views regarding autistic people. This was a word I had not heard of before and, in a short space of time, I realized that it is the positive path to take in an oppressive, medically dominated world. The neurodiversity perspective is the perspective everybody needs. In this book, I share the things I wish I had known about autism and the global autistic community.

When I talk about the spectrum, I do not necessarily mean the *autistic* spectrum, as it is so misunderstood. The global community is the spectrum! Autistic people do not necessarily have a specific place *on* this spectrum, we are all in it together!

Given that I am a prolific writer, I decided to catalog and document questions that I was asked at book signings and during my speaking tours. This is a collection of the most frequently asked questions from parents, professionals, and autistics themselves. I answer these from a unique position, in that I am both autistic and a professional, in the hope that it will inspire autistic people and their parents at all stages in life, from awaiting a diagnosis to thriving in the workplace as a proud autistic adult.

I want everyone to read this book and be inspired not only by my perspective and how I got through life but by how other autistic people have done so, too. We can do it! We have made it and, most important, we change and contribute to the world every day. It's a path that goes from childhood to university, the workplace, and beyond. If I can do it, you can too!

The learning journey is never over. In that respect, I identify with one of my literary heroes, Zarathustra:

> "I am a wanderer and a mountain climber, he said to his heart. I do not like the plains and it seems I cannot sit still for long. And whatever may come to me now as destiny and experience—it will involve wandering and mountain climbing: ultimately one experiences only oneself."[1]

# 1

# Who Made You the Messiah to These Lost Souls?

I decided to write *Loving Your Place on the Spectrum* to answer some of the most frequently asked questions from both personal and professional perspectives. I am autistic and I am a social worker, which means that I live on both sides of the divide that exists between the community and professionals. I am not an expert just because I am autistic, although I live and breathe autism every day of my life. It is who I am. I am among those who have found their voice and advocate for our community. After years of struggle, I found my voice and have dedicated it to sharing the perspectives of my community, and myself, in ways that contribute to the betterment of all.

Throughout *Loving Your Place on the Spectrum*, I use my autistic voice and bring in the voices of other autistic people to share the challenges we face. I am only one autistic person, but there are so many more out there of all genders, ages, beliefs, and mind-sets. This isn't a guidebook, this isn't an instructional manual, but more of an inspirational guide like what one would use when they want to know what furniture to put in their house or where they want to go for a holiday!

Advocacy isn't easy. It's fraught with challenges. When I started to campaign for autistic people I was met with some opposition. It's a process of listening and learning from others in the community, their families and friends, the professionals and counselors who help them, and the employers who provide them work. If I truly hear what each has to contribute, I am capable of moving my advocacy forward, allowing both the community and the general population to better understand themselves and each other.

I have gathered a fine collection of stories from the autistic community, which I am proudly part of, to give a general overview of how being autistic isn't easy. As children, we must conform to the practices that make others most comfortable, and as adults that doesn't change so much. If anything, I have learned that being in a classroom and being in a workplace environment are pretty much the same thing. A lot of our experiences are terribly similar at all stages of life and it comes down to one thing: misunderstanding.

At some stage, people will ask you about being autistic. I wanted to include some of the questions I was asked whenever I spoke to groups, schools, or conferences. I have spoken not only at formal events but also informally with other autistic advocates, and they told me that they were asked very similar questions. A lot of the time, I was asked these questions without having a pre-prepared answer, and I wanted to outline the answers here that I wish I had given at the time. Hopefully, these will inspire you to find your own answers, no matter your age or if you are in school or the workforce.

## Where Are You on the Autistic Spectrum?

Many books are marketed as useful tools to teach others about the autistic spectrum and how they can help you better understand it.

This isn't necessarily accurate or functional. The autistic spectrum is a huge thing! It isn't a sliding scale of severity in the same way cancer is viewed. It doesn't progress from stage 1 to stage 2. One cannot be higher or lower on the spectrum than someone else. I am not lower on the spectrum, and someone with a learning disability isn't higher. That isn't the way it is. There are so many things that make autistic people unique, hence the term spectrum instead of scale.

I suppose I can empathize with killer whales in that they aren't whales but the largest member of the dolphin family. It is common misnomers, as well as outdated ideas and prejudices, that make being autistic more difficult than the "symptoms" of autism that have been outlined in many mainstream autistic-cause websites and books. It's like the visible light spectrum, where one color isn't more important than the other. Red isn't more serious than green, despite being on two different ends of the spectrum. They coexist together as one colorful community, as do we.

If I were to write a generic guidebook about the autistic spectrum and what one should do in every situation, it would be universally condemned and an insult to all of us. The spectrum is much too broad to be able to give specific advice and guidance that would fit every single person within it. I will give a prime example: If there is one thing in the world that saddens me more than discrimination, it is the feeling of sand on my bare feet. I always wear my shoes on the beach and this is completely non-negotiable.

When I said this to a group I was speaking to, a parent told me that her son absolutely loved the feeling of sand on his feet and it brought him great calm and peace. In my mind, this little boy was completely wrong and in no circumstance should anyone have to experience the horror of sand between their toes. Does this mean that I am higher on the spectrum than this child? No, it doesn't. We exist perfectly on the spectrum together although we both have differing sensory likes and dislikes. Just because one has a sensory preference that doesn't fit with what would be perceived as "the norm," it doesn't mean that it justifies a higher ranking on the spectrum. If anyone is to take anything away from this book, let it be that!

## Realizing You Are Autistic, the "WOW Moment"

The self-acceptance journey for autistic people is one that not many understand. Recognizing and accepting that you are autistic is not an instantaneous realization, even when medical doctors have labeled you as such. It isn't a sudden turning point in life, nor is it one that instantly comes into reality. It takes time to reach acceptance. My journey has taken an entire twenty-five years and, it is safe to say, this journey is still very much in progress. I went through the mainstream school system as an autistic child, which was something very radical and new in the mid-1990s. Had I been born ten or more years earlier, I probably would have had to go to a special education school, despite the fact that I had a high IQ and demonstrated academic ability.

I can empathize with so many autistic people as I, like them, went through a lot of similar hardships as a young boy and as a man. I often sat in my classroom and wondered why I had to have a classroom assistant with me everywhere I went. I knew in my mind that I was just as capable as everyone else in my class; I just liked to do things differently. I would sit in the classroom and wonder why people did things in the manner that they did. If we were making collages as a group, I was totally dumbfounded as to why people would use glue; it sticks to your fingers and it's terribly difficult to wash off! Why can't people just use tape? Or when we were doing active physical activities, I couldn't stand the sound of squeaking shoes against the natural echo of the hall we were in. And when I decided I wanted no part in something, like using glue for a collage, it was incredibly difficult to persuade me otherwise.

All of these types of experiences combined to make me very bitter inside. My classmates were able to cope with things that I very clearly could not cope with. Many believe, often incorrectly, that autistic children have no understanding or concept of the world around them. I can't speak for every single autistic person, but I know that this wasn't the case for me. When I went home from school, I often wondered why I wasn't like everyone else. I sat in my room and felt like I was somehow diseased, different and not worthy of anything. I knew some of my teachers didn't want me in their classroom and I knew I had been excluded from some birthday parties. I wasn't oblivious to these facts, even as a small child, and they hurt me deeply.

This isn't a feeling that is easy to shake off. It was like a snowball effect right through my life. The scars from primary school carried over into secondary school and the scars from secondary school carried over into adulthood. By early adulthood I knew I was autistic. This served as the "wow moment" as to why I was so different than everybody else. From my earliest memory, I knew I was different. My diagnosis came when I was eleven and, because I was so young, my parents wanted to protect me and struggled with whether or not they should tell me I was autistic. They actually told me when I was nineteen and it brought a sense of closure for me that came in two opposite forms: it did answer my question of why I was so different but it also made me feel a sense of shame that closed me off from the world.

It took a lot of time, courage, and self-sacrifice to come to terms with being autistic and to begin the journey of letting go. I didn't want to admit defeat but I felt that if I accepted help, I somehow would have felt that I was broken, damaged and in need of repair. Many autistic people I have spoken to in the writing process for this book felt the same way.

## Why Did You Tell Your Story?

As children, many of us struggled to find our voice or communicate in a way that made everyone around us understand. After diagnosis, many turn to the internet to ask all of life's questions. Many, including me, wanted to know more about the autistic label. All I saw online were websites that said we were "loners" and "found it difficult to make friends" and had "obsessive and repetitive patterns of behavior." It can be a constant battle, and having to read so many negative stereotypes can be disheartening.

People who do not have direct knowledge of autism will rely on negative stereotypes that have been well publicized but may not be factual for everyone living in the autistic community. Does this mean we should sit back and accept that? Absolutely not! We must use our voices to explain that we are not and should not be categorized by the negative stereotypes bestowed upon us by the non-autistic majority. It simply is not fair. The only way this will stop is if you tell your story. It doesn't matter what medium you use, whether it be written, verbal, or through music, art, photography, or even dance! We have a duty to ourselves and to other autistic people out there, so that we may live happy and successful lives.

Having a voice isn't simply the ability to speak or communicate verbally. So many autistic people communicate and express themselves through other mediums like those listed above. I always loved reading and writing, and I decided that I would write a book of my own that told my story. Having connected with so many more people in the autistic community, I realized there are other stories told in different ways. I have met some incredible autistic artists, musicians, speakers, and more. All their stories have the same message: we can do great things!

## Finding My Voice

Having gone on the acceptance journey of my own, I decided to write about it. I would love to say that I wrote my first book with the sole intention of inspiring autistic people around the globe, but that wasn't the reason in the beginning. My son, Ethan, was starting to realize that I am not like him and that I like to do things in a certain way at home. Ethan would always wonder why our shoes occupy a particular spot in the house and why I don't like too many lights on at the same time. These were questions from a six-year-old that I was not able to answer very easily, so I decided to write my story down so that he could read it when he was a little bit older.

Ethan had just started school and his experience was completely different than mine. He has lots of friends, is full of fun, and doesn't have a classroom assistant. To demonstrate our differences, I wanted to provide an accurate record of what the early lives of Ethan and myself were like. I sat down to write the story of my life from the age of three up until I was twenty-six.

This became my little project. I love giving myself tasks and projects as an outlet for my boundless passion and enthusiasm. I had always wanted to have a book written and published by the time I was thirty and I decided to seize the opportunity and write it. I completed the writing and typing of the book in one hundred days and, like any author, I decided that I would have a cover made and try to get it published.

I sent the manuscript to literary agents and I received a ton of rejection letters. Nobody wanted it! I read one particular letter that outlined in great detail that autism books were abundant and that the market was already saturated. I realized that my book was not the usual autism book. Typically, a parent writes about their autistic child but I wrote it about myself for my non-autistic son.

Not being one to accept defeat very easily, I kept trying literary agents and publishers. I could paper all my walls with these rejection letters and did not find an agent or publisher on the first attempt. I drew up a plan. I decided to self-publish and market the book myself, so that I could at least recoup the costs that went into the cover design and editing. I reached out to local autism groups to generate interest and to let them know that there is a story written by an autistic person.

Luckily, the response was fantastic and I self-published *Why Does Daddy Always Look So Sad?* on the 13th of May 2019. After climbing the sales charts, selling thousands of books, and gaining quite a bit of media traction, I was asked to visit a local group to sign books and answer questions from parents and group members. I was initially very hesitant to do this, as I didn't know what kind of questions I would be asked or what potential criticism I would come up against. There are instances in the book where I don't necessarily portray myself in a positive light. That is not due to the fact that I am autistic; it is simply because I couldn't accept it and I made many counterproductive decisions to avoid accepting myself. Understanding and accepting oneself is difficult.

When I eventually decided to visit this group, I felt at home right away. The group members were like me and I was like them. I loved that so many teenagers in the group read my story and that it had inspired them to understand that being autistic was okay! It was then that I realized that I didn't want autistic kids to harbor the same shame of being autistic as I did. Although I had written a book for Ethan, many people resonated with it and drew inspiration from it. This was an incredible by-product of the book and it made me feel a huge sense of pride that I had shared my story. After visiting one group, I was invited to visit other groups in what then became my "The Autistic Revolution" tour of Ireland. I loved meeting with organizations, professionals, and schools and speaking at some conferences. It is an exhilarating experience to confidently tell your story to those who need to hear it. I wished I'd had the same form of inspiration when I was young.

For every autistic person deciding if they should tell their story or not tell it, you never know whom you will inspire in the future. After a lot of media coverage and a proven track record of sales, I was picked up by my current agent and publisher. The book was re-released by Beyond Words in April 2020.

## What Is the Hardest Part of Being an Advocate?

The one thing many realize when they have told their story or made themselves known as autistic is the incredible lack of knowledge the general public has on the subject. With a trademark sprinkling of naïvety, I believed that my life would become infinitely easier and everyone would automatically understand and accept me. The moment I knew that I would have to make peace with my childhood in order to progress in adulthood wasn't the end of my story by any means.

During the speaking tours I was asked many difficult questions. Some people had their hearts in the right place and others were steeped in sheer ignorance and denial. The idea that an autistic person would be able to stand in front of a room full of people and speak was a baffling concept to most and led to the first challenging question.

## How, If You Are Autistic, Can You Speak in Front of All These People?

This is a question that I am asked repeatedly, and it gives me the perfect opportunity to discuss my pre-speech/interview ritual. A lot of autistic performers have rituals, and I like sharing mine. This is not a guide on how to stand on a stage and speak, but it does let the public know that some of us have rituals and it is absolutely fine to have a ritual if it makes you feel comfortable. I write my speeches and talks out by hand. Then I practice in front of a full-length mirror in my house so that I can view my hand gestures, movements, and facial expressions as I speak. Often, this process is repeated at least twenty times to ensure my timing is correct.

I am not one to stand at a podium or on one spot when I am speaking, although for my TEDx talk, I had to try to stand still, which, for me, was an incredibly difficult process. Eventually I was able to remain in one spot, but it isn't my usual style. When I arrive at a venue, I ask to go on the stage before the audience arrives so that I can acclimatize to my surroundings. I stand on the middle of the stage and calculate how many steps I can take, left, right, forward, and back. I find out how many steps I can take from one end of the stage to the other so that I don't stop talking when I am moving across the stage.

I also ask the sound and lighting engineers to shine the spotlight on me and give them an idea of where I am going to be at a particular part of the show. I have been told that being a lighting engineer at one of my talks is exhausting! After my pre-speech ritual, I am completely prepared to be introduced and walk onstage to face and greet the audience. It doesn't matter if I am meeting a group on their premises or if I am speaking in a theater, I always do these things; they are my rituals.

I prepare meticulously for absolutely everything. Going with the flow or improvisation does not compute in my brain. It's important for me to be completely prepared for absolutely everything in life, at least as much as humanly possible. Organization is important to me.

This question of capability and achievement when one is autistic doesn't only apply to me or relate to when I speak to people. Many autistic people say they are asked why they can do a particular thing. The common view of autism includes the inability to accomplish normal life tasks, much less specific projects. That preconceived idea is unfortunate and generally inaccurate. Autistic people can achieve anything and everything they want to achieve. In fact, many people, including some neuroscientists, speculate that Einstein was on the spectrum because he fit the stereotypical mainstream ideas of what that might mean. I would love to see Einstein's reaction if somebody asked him, "How, if you are autistic, did you manage to discover the nature of time, space, and reality?"

I took this question very personally on the few occasions it was asked of me, and I discovered that there were much deeper connotations to such a question. It comes from a mind-set that autistic people cannot do particular things. The misconception is that autistic people are often shy and retiring and don't like mixing with people very much.

I do fit in with that stereotype in some ways. I am not a fan of parties, social gatherings, or situations where a lot of conversations are going on at once. I find it very hard to follow multiple discussions or identify an opening in which to join a conversation, but speaking publicly is a very different situation. I can practice and rehearse what I expect to happen and how I want to present my words and myself. I am in complete control of the interaction that I have with the audience. In fact, I almost find it much easier to speak to a full theater than to speak to one person whom I may bump into on the street.

## Are You Using Autism as an Excuse?

I have not encountered a single autistic person who has not been accused of telling people they are autistic in order to avoid doing something that is outside their comfort zone. An example of this came up during the COVID-19 pandemic. Many countries and US states set guidelines for face covering and social distancing. Protocols explicitly outlined that autistic people would be exempt from wearing face coverings in public places. Given my occupation as a social worker who visits vulnerable people, I knew I had to wear a face covering while I was with them. I did find it difficult, but not as difficult as being on the receiving end of disapproving frowns from the public when I wasn't wearing a mask.

When I told people about my exemption from wearing a face covering, I was often asked if I was being difficult or if I was capitalizing on the fact that I am autistic so that I did not have to wear one. This could not have been further from the truth. Many sensory-restrictive things are things that I actually want to do! I would love to have been able to wear a mask all the time, everywhere I went, and I salute those who can break through the comfort barrier and wear one at all times. Because of the questions, I was left feeling guilty that I was somehow at fault for not complying with the mask requirements. I felt like a naughty little boy who was somehow rebelling against authority in the face of a global pandemic.

Then I realized that I wasn't the problem. The problem, as I came to see it, was the judgmental people who glared at me with disdain. Nobody can tell if a person is autistic just by looking at him or her. Simply based on how they look, you can't tell if a person has exemptible conditions such as bronchitis, chronic obstructive pulmonary disease (COPD), congestive heart failure, or asthma. The autistic community also falls into that category. People make uninformed judgments.

Change requires knowledge and understanding. An example is that I don't always have a problem with crowded bars or concerts, but I know other autistic people who do. I love music so I don't categorize the volume of the music as a sensory trigger. Those who don't like music do find it generates a reaction. If there is a sensory-sensitive autistic person with a group of friends, it can be embarrassing to explain why they don't want to attend a concert simply because the music and lights make them uncomfortable. We need to learn to state what bothers us, and people need to respect our words.

## We Are All a Little Bit Autistic, Right?

In my view, if we were all "a little bit autistic," the world would be a much better place. People would be much more understanding of each other and no one would be encouraged to do any number of things they didn't want to do.

There are people who believe that everyone is on the autistic spectrum and that we each experience things differently. I can see this viewpoint and why people think it is valid, but that doesn't make it correct or any less insulting. Being autistic is similar to being pregnant: you are or you are not. There is no in-between. When I have told people that I am autistic, the response is often, "Sure, everyone is a bit autistic." I am not a neuroscientist or an expert by any means, but I know one thing is true: to say that everyone is autistic belittles those who actually are autistic.

As an example, imagine a country experiencing a terrible drought and famine. Millions of people are displaced, children are starving, the economy has collapsed, and communities are filled with crime. In a discussion with someone from the country that is suffering, would you say, "Sure, we have all felt hunger and thirst, right?" That is a question that minimizes the catastrophic effect the famine and drought had in that country.

This lack of sensitivity shouldn't happen with anyone, including autistic people, who often view that type of attitude as very confusing to interpret and understand. Many autistics spend their life wondering why they are different. To them it is not logical when they are told that everyone is the same. If everyone were truly the same, one section of society, the majority, would not marginalize the autistic minority. Unfortunately, it sometimes seems that the overwhelming majority will pick on any minority, regardless of neurotype, skin color, sexual orientation, or nationality. This is a sad interpretation of society but one that should be carefully examined by all people.

## Because You Are Autistic, Do You Think You Are Suited to the Job You Do?

Many autistic people work in science, technology, engineering, and mathematics (STEM) careers. I don't work in such a career. Because I do not have a career that involves sitting alone in a small laboratory, my chosen profession somehow minimizes the fact that I am autistic in the eyes of some. I relate to the fact that some people find it difficult to understand that I am a social worker, especially when I write and speak about how difficult it can be for me to relate to other people. It seems to be a widely held belief that autistic people do not work well with the general public and, instead, lurk in the shadows because they are not capable of mixing or associating with others. I suppose there are various forms of media to blame this on, but we can't assign blame to everything. If we did, we would then become part of the problem.

When I graduated as a social worker, my professional choice and I were both met with mixed reactions. Those who truly believed in me knew I could do it. Those who didn't know much about autism, or me, didn't. Some colleagues questioned my ability to pick up on the nuance of non-verbal cues or my ability to truly understand people's feelings. I wonder if anyone really ever does that anyway. But, it is plainly obvious when people are in distress, in crisis, or vulnerable compared to others in society who are not.

I learned very quickly to play to my strengths. This can apply to any autistic person in any job! In fact, it can apply to every human being. I am very good at gathering information about a situation, dissecting it, peeling back all the layers, and then making a sound decision on what should be done. It has served me well and will continue to do so. Society may evolve and legislation may change but, no matter how evolution or changes occur, this skill will always serve me.

All people have to do is identify their particular strengths and what makes them thrive in life and the workplace and then they simply need to apply it. A strengths-based approach in life is always much more beneficial than focusing on the negative or adverse path. An example of this is how I hate the loud and incessant rumblings of hospitals. People think hospitals are quiet and calm but to me they aren't. I hear the constant squeaking of shoes on the floor, the rattling and beeping of medical equipment; I smell the overpowering odor of sterilization agents and see medics rushing around. All combined makes this a sensory hell for me. Whether I am working or not, I try to be in hospitals as little as possible. Knowing this about myself, I avoid setting myself up for failure by avoiding irritating situations, ones that feel uncomfortable to me from a sensory point of view, when possible.

## Who Made You the Messiah to These Lost Souls?

When I was asked this question, it really shook me. I have always been keen to educate myself on any challenges that any community faces, not just the autistic community. I suppose this is the social worker side of me coming out. I never saw myself as an innovator of thought or somehow leading the charge to educate people or change their minds about what being autistic is and means.

My answer at the time was, "Nobody. I simply tell my own story about how being autistic is okay and that I'd wished I had someone like me to draw inspiration from and to reassure me."

This was one of the questions that had a lingering effect on me long after the talk had ended. Do people really view autistic people as "lost souls"? In the past, I may have resented the fact I was autistic, but never at any stage did my parents believe I was a lost cause or overly worthy of pity. To me, there never is, and never was, a lost cause in humanity. There are only those who don't understand the struggles of others.

I thought long and hard as to whom the lost souls actually were, and then one day it hit me. It isn't the autistic community, it isn't parents of autistic children, and it isn't professionals with their hearts in the right place. To me the lost souls are those who still hold judgmental misconceptions about the autistic community. I have been known to ask teachers and professionals what autism is to them before I explain what it is to me. Of course, I get the same cookie-cutter answers: lack of eye contact, repetitive behaviors, and so on. Those are some of the things that are measured against non-autistic people. It should not be taught that not making eye contact is bad manners, if the child can't do it. The fact that children are still made to do this makes me quite sad. When I ask for educators to list the positive traits of autism, many discuss the passion, drive, and intellect of their autistic pupils and family members. I always follow those comments of approval with, "Why wasn't this discussed in the very beginning?"

Many autistic people are quite happy in their own skin, but according to others we shouldn't be. How does that make us lost souls? I don't want to be viewed as a messiah. I never wanted fame. But if telling my story and changing perceptions makes life easier for one autistic person, none of this will have been in vain. I feel a sense of duty to tell my story so that others can draw inspiration and tell their stories. I think that every autistic person needs to use their voice or medium of their choice to show the world that being autistic helps rather than hinders us.

I am an advocate for autism acceptance and I've learned how to be a communicator to and for everyone, whether they have direct knowledge or no knowledge at all of autism. The questions I get from others help me understand their needs. The value of their experiences and stories allows me to share with others that autism truly is a spectrum that cannot be encompassed by a "one size fits all" definition. We, like everyone else on this planet, are unique individuals. But, while most people celebrate their uniqueness, autistic people are diagnosed, labeled, and categorized. We are put into a uniform box that doesn't permit the growth and development that we, like everyone else, require. Discovering and understanding what that diagnosis means to each of us, as individuals, is important so that the autistic person may develop more fully.

This book is a glimpse into the challenges that I face when advocating not only for myself but also for other autistic people like me. Textbooks say that we resist change but I have discovered that when we use our voices to change the stereotypical, antiquated narratives that surround autism, we can adapt, broaden our horizons, and step out of that box that has confined us for so long.

# 2

# What Is Autism?

That is the million-dollar question: What is autism? With today's remarkable world of technology, all one must do is google that question and you will have access to more information than you can imagine or absorb. And a good deal of it is outdated and completely wrong! To build a foundation for the pages that follow, we need to define what autism is and, most important, what it is not.

Eugen Bleuler, a Swiss psychiatrist, first brought the word "autism" into mainstream use in 1910. Autism comes from the Greek word *autos*, which means "self." Bleuler used it to mean morbid self-admiration. Bleuler also coined the terms "schizoid" and "schizophrenia." In some respects, the Swiss psychiatrist was ahead of his time because he preferred that children and adults who struggled with mental health issues return to their families and communities to avoid institutionalization. On the other hand, he supported eugenic sterilization for those diagnosed with schizophrenia. Eugenic sterilization means that you selectively sterilize certain people to prevent them from having children who may also have symptoms of a mental illness, affliction, or what are viewed as poor characteristics for the human race.

Although autism as a word was first coined back at the beginning of the last century, there have been case studies documented from centuries before. *Table Talk* was a collection of Martin Luther's sayings that were transcribed by his students. Mathesius, one of the students, transcribed a story of a twelve-year-old child who was, most likely, autistic. Luther apparently thought the poor boy was "a soulless mass of flesh possessed by the devil" and recommended he be suffocated!

I bring up Martin Luther's drastic determination because differences in people have never really been accepted. Even before autism was a term or brought into common use, differences have been frowned upon and disparaged. Another well-documented story is that of the Wild Boy of Aveyron, a feral child captured by hunters in 1798. A medical student named Jean Itard took the child into his care and named him Victor. Itard wanted Victor to form social attachments to other people and tried to teach him to speak by utilizing a behavioral therapy program Itard created. Those who studied Victor hypothesized that his differences may have been the reason his parents abandoned him, forcing him to fend for himself in the wild. Itard tried to educate Victor by reading to him, introducing him to other people, and speaking with him for prolonged periods.

The written reports and literature of that era documented that Victor did many of the things associated with autistic people, like rocking back and forth, grinding his teeth, and sudden, sharp movements. It was clear to Itard that Victor wasn't deaf, but when several other scholars asked him why he didn't attempt to teach Victor sign language, Itard found it difficult to prove that Victor wasn't deaf. Victor did not readily respond to the spoken word. Victor's case prompted intense philosophical discussions based on what separates humans from animals. Itard adopted Victor and took him into his home. Victor did make some prog-ress, although his verbal speech was limited and he didn't progress beyond what would be defined, at that time, as a "rudimentary level." Victor passed away from pneumonia at the age of forty in 1828, never fully integrated into society as Itard had hoped.

As an autistic person, I feel a great deal of sympathy for Victor and what he experienced as someone different. Constantly being studied and evaluated is a sad and lonely way to grow up. I have been there, as have many others.

Autism became much more mainstream in 1938 when Hans Asperger, of the Vienna University Hospital, cited Bleuler's terminolo-gies in a lecture he named "Autistic Psychopaths." Asperger, of course, is the namesake of the diagnosis labeled Asperger's syndrome, which has since been incorporated into the overall diagnosis of autism. In fact, Asperger's syndrome didn't become a separate diagnosis until 1981. That is what I was diagnosed with back in 2001, but it is no longer in common usage as a medical diagnosis. Instead the term "autism" or "ASD" (autism spectrum disorder) is applied.

The first official diagnosis of autism was made in 1938; it was given to a little boy named Donald Triplett. Triplett displayed incredible musi-cal talent and could name notes as they were played to him on a piano. His dad described him as withdrawn but marveled at the child's math-ematical ability and the fact that he was able to recite biblical passages by the age of two. Triplett displayed incredible savant capabilities that inspired everyone around him.

Leo Kanner, of the Johns Hopkins Hospital, first used autism in a modern sense when he introduced the term "early infantile autism" in a 1943 study of eleven children.[1] He noted similar differences that were, in his words, "autistic aloneness" and "insistence on sameness" in the children. It is difficult for me to read these studies and realize that the doctors making these proclamations about autistic people know so very little about us. Some of us actually enjoy our own company and feel comfortable having structured days! To us this is not an affliction and it should not be judged as such. Since that early form of pathologizing, which means treating someone as psychologically unhealthy, the characterizations of autistic people have spiraled out of control. So here we are, left with the definition that presents the same concepts that were applauded almost a century ago. This definition of autism comes straight from the *Oxford English Dictionary*:

A developmental disorder of variable severity that is characterized by difficulty in social interaction and communication and by restricted or repetitive patterns of thought and behavior.

This very definition sets the tone for this entire book because this is how people like me are confined: stuck in a prefabricated commentary filled with degrading terms. We are so much more than that horrible and limiting definition. The words "disorder," "restricted," "difficulty," "severity," and "behavior" all combine to make an extremely damaging definition of what we, in the autistic community, believe makes us the wonderfully unique people that we are. It is a fact that we are autistic. How could anyone love their place on the spectrum if they are delineated in such demeaning terms? This dictionary's definition does one thing that is positive: it shines a huge spotlight on what autistic existence is like. It is, unfortunately, how the neurotypical or the "normal" majority view autistic people.

One thing I know for certain is that this definition, and similar descriptions, consolidates the existing reason for the low self-image that I felt when I was younger and so many others feel, as well. No matter what method one employs to learn about autism, the only descriptive highlights are all the negative things such as lack of eye contact, obsessing over trivial things, and preferring to be alone. What saddens me is that individuals and groups whose primary objective is to support autistic people often voice these defamatory depictions. I do not see how that assists the autistic community, and I can't help but wonder if, maybe, they just don't know better.

I cannot approach the topics that follow in this book without highlighting one thing in particular: autistic people do struggle in some areas. I am not saying that autistic people do not need support; often they do. But we, the autistic community, would greatly benefit from society being in a more positive space and better educated when it comes to autism. I know from my social work background that in many countries, a diagnosis is needed to access services, support, and even welfare. Why is all of that necessary? I have had the honor and privilege of speaking to hundreds if not thousands of autistic people, and their parents, from all around the world. I have never met anyone who has believed themselves or their child to be autistic and been wrong about their personal diagnosis. My own parents weren't wrong, although not many, if any, support systems existed when I was growing up in the 1990s and 2000s. A formal diagnosis only serves to tell people what they already know. When help is needed it is needed.

Like a bad case of cognitive association, the very word "autism" seems to generate fear among some people. When clinicians diagnose small children as autistic, the clinician tends to apologize, and parents' worries grow. Fear hampers anyone's growth and development. I hope this isn't going to be the case much longer. In time, I hope that we can remove the association between autism and fear by shifting the definition of autism to one that allows each of us to develop and mature as unique individuals, just like everyone else. How can this be achieved? There are many ways but we can begin when children are diagnosed.

Parents can be positive and hopeful for the future and not allow the seeds of despair to grow into giant trees of fear.

Autism is a loaded word and often used in the wrong context. From my travels and discussions with other people, autism seems to be a word that is used to define those who have intellectual disabilities. Yes, it is true that those with intellectual disabilities can be autistic but autism is not an intellectual disability in and of itself. Autistic people simply view and interact with the world differently. I always thought *the way I perceived* the world and everything that happened in it was wrong and needed to change. This is a common experience. Autistic adults who reflect on their childhood usually say they felt that the way they were was wrong, simply because they didn't see things like everyone else.

## The Medical Model of Disability

The medical model of disability focuses on three main things: diagnosing, treating, and eventually curing. Physical illnesses also fit within the boundaries of the medical model. If someone is diagnosed with cancer, it is imperative that medical treatment is sought in order to maintain quality of life or enter remission entirely. It makes perfect sense and I don't believe many would disagree with this pathway when it comes to cancer or any other debilitating illness or disease. But disabilities, and especially autism, are different.

In 1980, the World Health Organization (WHO) released a template that focused on disability. It is called the "International Classification of Impairments, Disabilities, and Handicaps." (Although in common usage, the word "handicap" is a huge no-no.) The framework seeks to approach the subject of disability by using the terms outlined in the title of the document.

The WHO described impairment as "any loss or abnormality of psychological, physiological, or anatomical structure or function."[2] Disability is described as "any restriction or lack (resulting from an impairment) of ability to perform an activity in the manner or within the range considered normal for a human being."[3]

The word "normal" comes up quite often. I always wonder who decides what is "normal" or who conceptualizes it as the yardstick with which every individual is measured. The medical model does cover all ailments, physical and cognitive. A key issue arises when it comes to autism and autistic people, because a lot of us don't see ourselves as disabled, nor do we want a cure or to be treated in any way.

I have been asked if I view myself as disabled. That is not how I see myself, nor is it the description many other autistic people use as a self-definition. We believe we just have a different operating system from the people who created the "normal" yardstick. It shouldn't be surprising that many autistic people share the same sentiment as me. Of course, autistic people with the simultaneous presence of two or more intellectual disabilities will require much higher levels of care and support than a lot of us.

Ultimately, the medical model focuses on the limitations autistic people have. Much of the medical research money is used to determine what causes autism in order to eventually reach a determination of how autistic people can be cured, made "normal," or, at least, made to appear to fit in with society. What is often overlooked is that many of us are very capable of thriving in society. However, because of the desire to change us, we are unfairly labeled with terms such as "non-compliant" or "defiant." We are left believing that our own ways of achieving the same result are deemed wrong by the normal ones.

Some terms are very strongly associated with the medical model. One of them is that people "have" autism. Saying someone "has" autism generates the same thinking pattern as when someone says they have a profoundly serious physical illness. Having a serious illness is different. Autism is something that cannot be treated and removed or cured. It is something that is part of us from birth. From a medical stand-point, doctors and clinicians know that people cannot separate from their neurology.

I do not want to sound like an autism supremacist who has a naïve and very unrealistic view of what autistic people are. We do have our struggles, just like every other group of people. We face obstacles that are not of our making but exist nonetheless. To the outside world, these difficulties may seem insurmountable, and if the outside world is try-ing to make us fit into their definition of normal, they are right; it's overwhelming. However, it is much easier to understand if they simply view the obstacles before us as different than what they are used to because our issues just happen to be different than what they may have to deal with in their lives. They would be quite surprised to see that we who are autistic can thrive and participate in society by bringing our talents to the world stage. We don't have to be just like them in order to fit into their world. We would just like to be accepted for who we are.

In the view of many in the autistic community, the medical model, though well-intentioned, has had the unintended effect of socially degrading an entire group of people. Their hearts may be in the right place, but when someone tries to change a child, it can leave emotional scars that can last throughout life. The pain may not show physically, but it is there, in their heart and mind. The best way to equate it is this way: Imagine that your earliest memories consisted of being told that you have to change, that you don't do anything right, that you are inca-pable, and that if you don't change you will never be part of society. That is the experience of many autistic people.

## The Social Model of Disability

The social model of disability promotes a different approach when looking at disabilities. The main focus is to look for systemic barriers, exclusion (whether it is intentional or not intentional), and the overall attitudes of society toward certain categorizations of people. Disability in this context doesn't show what a person's individual body or mind can do or not do or accomplish. Instead it creates boundaries of what restrictions society places on people who are not like them. A social model of disability doesn't encourage individuals to change or get better. It does push society to change its attitudes.

Perhaps the best way to compare the medical model to the social model is this: someone can't climb a flight of stairs. The medical model would place a huge emphasis on helping that person climb the stairs, rather than looking at the glaringly obvious solution of removing the stairs and replacing them with a ramp, which would be the social model.

Another major difference between the medical model and the social model is "having autism," the medical designation, versus "being autistic," which aligns more with the social criteria. Autistic people generally prefer to say that they *are* autistic as opposed to "having autism." I understand this because *being* autistic is meaningful to me; it makes me who I am. It took me a long time to realize that fact and to love myself for it. Being autistic can be—and is—wonderful, and the last thing I want is for future generations of children to grow up being ashamed of who they are, like I did.

When I started writing about being autistic, I said that I had autism and that I had a "condition" and so on. I was, more or less, following the medical model of thought. I don't think it's unusual for autistic advocates to begin their advocacy journey using the same language I did. The medical model is so prevalent in common terminology that it is what most autistic people grow up with and accept as the norm, without realizing the impact that it has on our own feelings of self-worth and how society views us. I learned that my choice of language was offensive to autistic people. Of course, the offense wasn't intentional, but that doesn't negate how my words made others feel. When I was informed of the terminology preferred by the majority of autistic people, I honored and understood their choice of words and used them instead of the traditional verbiage. I accepted it and immediately began using it as the basis for my own thinking. I had been corrected and wanted to educate myself further. I learned that people outside the autistic community often dismissed voiced desires from those within the community, as if our preference for the words that describe us has no value. I learned from and admired the self-advocates who spoke up, made their feelings known, and informed me of their choice.

A word that is used to define oneself is very personal and should be accepted by others. Just the concept of saying someone "is autistic" instead of someone "has autism" presents a different response from non-autistic people. "Someone is autistic" says to the world that that person claims their autism. It is a matter of fact. "Someone has autism" creates the impression that that person is ill, incapable, or a victim. The majority of the autistic world prefers the former; we are autistic.

Autistic advocates all over the world, including me, are trying to change society's attitudes toward autistic people and autism itself. As a community, we are simply another diversity group that should be accepted, not hidden away, changed, or made to fit in with everyone else. The social model is a much more contemporary and progressive model that doesn't seek to alter everyone to be like the typical majority. It is much more accepting, but it does require that the "normal" people alter their thinking a bit.

## The Autistic Spectrum

The autistic spectrum is easily one of the most, if not the most, misunderstood aspects of the entire topic of autism and neurodiversity. The autistic spectrum is generally recognized as a scale of severity, like a sliding scale that goes from left to right with "less severe" on one end and "more severe" on the other end. The spectrum is wrongly used to determine the severity of someone's autism. This isn't how it should be viewed. The only way autistic people thrive is when people understand, appreciate, and accept them and their self-identity.

Think of the autistic spectrum as a circle where different people can fit anywhere within it. Different people have different sensory preferences and needs, different levels of motor skills, and different levels of logic and problem solving. Some may have very high sensory needs but incredibly fine motor skills. We are all there; different but equal. That's what makes the circular image of the autistic spectrum so inclusive and vibrant.

Some people might disagree with this, as many have told me that their child had a certain "level" of autism when they were diagnosed. A majority of those families that were told of their child's "level of autism" were in the United States. I think that has a lot to do with the two different health systems between the UK/Ireland and the United States. The UK National Health Service is free and the American system is an insurance-based, for-profit system. Assigning levels, as is often done in the US, is a method of determining what therapies will be applied to the child. I am as autistic now as I was when I was born; your child will be too. But the US medical model, and others, determines what therapy is best based on their scales of diagnosis.

With the antiquated spectrum logic, I would be seen as "low on the spectrum" simply because I have a family, a car, a house, and a job and can stand on a stage in front of large crowds. I wasn't "low on the spectrum" when I seemed to be withdrawn in school because I felt I didn't fit in. I wasn't "low on the spectrum" when I was waiting for my son to be born, and I certainly will not be "low on the spectrum" if I lose someone I love. The autistic spectrum shouldn't be viewed like the IQ scale that states that 70 or below is verging on intellectual disability and 140 is genius. We cannot be defined on a linear scale. I have met people with lower IQs that function very well in society, and those who have a very high IQ that may not function as well as would be expected. That's why it is a circle of very different, very unique individuals who just happen to not fit into the mold of "normal."

## Neurodiversity

The term "neurodiversity" was born in 1998 when Judy Singer, an Australian sociologist, teamed up with American reporter Harvey Blume. This was the first mainstream perspective that society's views of what are described as "neurodevelopmental disorders" are more aligned with the medical model even though some of us prefer acceptance rather than a cure. Neurodiversity was used to define the multitude of ways in which the human mind and brain can work when it comes to attention span, mood, sociability, and other mental functions.

Neurodiversity is a model that is closely aligned with the autistic community and autism itself, although there are variants of differences that are encapsulated in the concept of neurodiversity, such as ADHD and dyslexia. Neurodiversity advocates tirelessly promote that being different is perfectly okay. I agree and I salute every single advocate that encourages the positives of being autistic. We each have different talents and abilities, such as having a good memory, musical talent, creativity, and remarkable attention to detail, all of which are constructive.

Another term that meets with opposition from the community is "autism spectrum disorder" (ASD). ASD refers to the diagnostic part of being autistic. When someone asks me if I have ASD, I respond, "Disordered compared to whom?"

Neurodiversity takes some very strong stances on certain topics such as finding a cause or something to blame for autism, which falls under the medical model. Neurodiversity rejects this, and (I feel) rightfully so. Most of us in the autistic community prefer to look forward and progress rather than be subjected to the constraints and restrictions of the medical model. Even if they uncovered and proved that something did cause autism, it wouldn't matter to us because autism would still create the wonderful individuals that we are. I am proud of myself and of being autistic, and I want others to see and experience that feeling. Wondering why and how come a person is autistic doesn't improve that person's life or the life of anyone in that family. Neurodiversity urges parents of autistic children to channel their concerns into nurturing energy that allows them to accept their child, without blame or guilt. That loving acceptance will only cause your already wonderful child to develop more fully.

Did you know that a puzzle piece was the first global symbol that identified autistic people? It was first used in the United Kingdom in 1963 as the logo for the National Autistic Society (NAS). A puzzle piece was chosen to represent the puzzling aspects of autism. NAS has since changed their logo, but the puzzle piece is still recognized internationally as a symbol of autism. It certainly raised awareness of autism and the challenges associated with it. However, the puzzle piece's connotation is confusing in itself. The meaning isn't entirely clear and might denote several things. Does the puzzle piece mean that we have a piece missing? Does it mean that we don't fit into the bigger picture? Does it mean that we are puzzling? I don't find that I am comfortable with any of those limiting possibilities.

Neurodiversity has adopted a new symbol. It's on the cover of this book: the gold infinity symbol. This is a much more friendly symbol. The infinity symbol means that the possibilities for us are both endless and limitless. The gold color represents the chemical symbol for gold, which is Au, which also happens to be the first two letters of *Autistic*. I haven't found anyone who is offended by the infinity symbol and hope that it becomes the universally recognized symbol of the autistic community. We are gold!

## Autism Awareness

Many people in the world have participated in "autism awareness" training. What does it make them aware of? As a social worker, I've attended this type of training and it promotes the medical model and the negative associations that surround autism and autistic people. When I give live talks, I like to tell everyone that I am about to talk about autism awareness and then ask everyone to raise their hand if they have heard of the term "autism." When every hand in the room or theater is raised, I tell them that my job is done and turn as if I am going to leave the stage.

Obviously, this book is for autistic people, family and friends of autistic people, and teachers, aides, and others who work with autistic people. But this book is also for anyone who doesn't know what autism is or has never been touched by it. Through my experiences and the experiences of other autistic people, *Loving Your Place on the Spectrum* will tell you what being autistic is really like, not what others think it might be like. The days of raising awareness are over; what we all need to do now is work toward acceptance and inclusion.

## Autistic Issues and Awareness

Although many autistic people have brought the neurodiversity model to the table, there are still some unsettling facts that remain. Very few autistic people are employed, and it isn't necessarily because they are unemployable. If an employer were to look up autism in the dictionary, the definition would most likely deter them from hiring an autistic person. It even knocks the confidence of autistic people, sometimes to the point that they don't want to find work!

Confidence and self-esteem are huge issues for us. I used to express a false type of confidence that is called "masking." As a teenager, I wouldn't let my vulnerabilities show to other people because I didn't fully know or appreciate who I was. I have improved my skills (like communicating) as I have more life experience, to the point that sometimes I have been rightfully accused of oversharing! I really don't see that as a negative; it is much better than keeping everything stuffed inside. This is one of those things we, the autistic community, need to develop as a skill. We need to be less concerned with what others may think of our communicative skills and utilize them to the best of our abilities.

There's a tremendous increase in initiatives to support autistic people, as well as their parents, siblings, aides, and teachers, in a variety of areas. The dollar amount that has been spent to offer support is amazing and commendable. The support is wonderful, but no one is asking us what we need. Instead we get what someone else thinks we need. Communication with groups supporting neurodiversity would help funnel the funds to areas that could assist autistic people in the ways they want to be supported.

We know we are not indistinguishable from our "normal" peers, and we don't always *want* to fit in with everyone else. We view the wonderful traits we have as something that makes us unique. In fact, many of us wonder why being neurotypical, or non-autistic, is so great. I don't have an answer to that question, and I don't know anyone who does. No one is perfect; we all have things we can improve and, most importantly, we can all learn to accept each other for who we are. Whether you're neurotypical or neurodiverse, we can all benefit from acceptance.

## Neurodiversity Training International (NTI)

The concept of neurodiversity has been around for decades, but not enough progress has been made to really propel it forward. This isn't due to the lack of voices from the autistic community speaking out, but rather the ears of society have not heard their voices. There are organizations that promote events to raise the awareness of autism. Sometimes these events are larger gatherings and sometimes they are as simple as morning coffee with a group, or a sponsored walk. I actually attended a couple of these. I went to a coffee morning in a local hotel that was seeking to raise funds for autism awareness. I always make an effort to attend any kind of training to improve my own knowledge and skills and utilize any opportunity to learn something different. I love to report what I've learned and share it with everyone I encounter. The first thing I had to discover was where the coffee morning was taking place. There was no sign at the hotel entrance. I asked around and found out that the coffee morning was on the second floor and I would have to sign in and make a donation at the door. I cordially gave my donation and proceeded into the room. The room itself was comprised entirely of adults. I didn't see any children there, not that children drink a lot of coffee. I learned very quickly that the coffee was cold and that the cake was both dry and dense. I learned that a colleague of mine was expecting a baby in four months and that the organizer's father had died suddenly and that she couldn't attend the coffee morning. There wasn't much chat about autism from the people I had talked to, so I decided to put my cup of cold coffee down and leave. I didn't learn anything about autism.

Several weeks later, I saw a poster that said a charity walk for autism was taking place near my home. I thought this would be a chance to learn more from people who are part of the autistic community, and their parents and friends. I decided to register so that I could acquaint myself with local groups and services and see what awareness would be raised. I turned up on the day with my fancy new sneakers, ready to devour the miles. A hearty walk was perfect because I wanted to start exercising again following my retirement from marathon running. It was a very cold day, and the clouds overhead were about to open up and pour down rain on everyone. I'd brought my son, Ethan, with me; he'd donned his rainproof jacket and boots and was looking forward to the adventure with Dad. As Ethan and I walked with the masses of people, we happened to learn that a new café had opened near our home and we agreed that we would have to go there for a lunch date. That was the extent of what I learned that day. (And yes, it started to rain halfway through the route.)

Numerous events have the "autism awareness" tag on them but don't really teach or demonstrate anything about autistic people. In both cases, if someone told me that I had come to a retirement coffee morning and a peaceful march, I would have been none the wiser. These groups are missing opportunities when there are large gatherings of people. Autism awareness groups are designed to bring information to both the neurodiverse and neurotypical communities. People like educators, medical professionals, parents, and family members attend these events. These group events have the perfect chance to live up to their names and present autism awareness as a showcase for all the amazing things that make us the diverse group that we are. If there were more "acceptance" events as opposed to "awareness" events, people might actually learn something. The offshoot of those two experiences was my founding and creation of Neurodiversity Training International (NTI). NTI is designed to nourish and spread acceptance of the autistic community and reinforce the gifts and pride of being an autistic person.

I love linguistics and language structures. I am proficient in both French and Spanish. When I prepare a speech, I look up the words and definitions for autism in other languages. I recently came upon a wonderful definition in the Maori language. The word they coined for autism is *takiwatanga*, which means "in his/her own time and space." This describes us. We exist in our own time and space. I thought it was an incredibly moving definition that can expand the acceptance of autistic people.

This, to me, hones the point that the definition of autism can be easily changed or recreated and doesn't have to be limiting, confining, or derogatory. *Takiwatanga* is an expansion of thought, much like neurodiversity, which isn't about being divisive, but is about being inclusive.

I created NTI because I dream of a world that adopts neurodiversity so that autistic people are better understood and appreciated, given support and guidance when and where it is needed. I believe that the autistic person should initiate the support that is provided. The way this process starts is to provide a platform that allows autistic people to tell their stories. I told mine and it has been a life-changing experience. Since then, I have gathered other stories, some of which I have shared within the pages of this book, along with my own experiences and thoughts.

My goal is to help the mainstream view of autism change. I want to see society broaden its definitions of autism to be more inclusive, more understanding, and more accepting of those who are different than they are. I hope that neurotypical and neurodiverse minds and hearts will be won over and an innovative and fresh view of autism established.

# 3

# I Believe Myself/My Child to Be Autistic; What Do I Do Next?

The individuals in my community are far too often characterized by distortions such as "all autistic children are less aware" and then, after the medical diagnosis, we are almost always told "the medics and professionals know best." After speaking with individuals and groups that have a personal involvement with autism, I'm inclined to believe that a medical diagnosis put a rubber stamp on what was already known, or at least suspected. I found that parents of autistic children recognized differences early on in the child's life, and those who were not diagnosed until they were adults always knew that they were very different.

An example of that lifelong awareness is from Evaleen Whelton, a speech and drama teacher whose focus has always been on positive self-image and confidence in children. With a degree in commerce from University College Cork in Ireland, she set up her business to help children believe in themselves, using drama as a tool to create opportunities for building confidence. This led her to set up another business, Konfident Kidz, where she developed programs to teach social skills through drama.

In 2017 Evaleen developed a training course to share her skills with parents and professionals, and her "Get Konnected Program" has been hugely successful. It's the first course of its kind designed to teach people about autistic communication and to coach autistic children, teens, and young adults on communication skills used by people who are not autistic. She then established AUsome Training and has been instrumental in changing the narrative around autism. Her work continues today and she is widely recognized for helping our community develop a positive self-image and respect for the beauty of our differences. Her website, konfidentkidz.ie, covers all her endeavors.

Evaleen calls her experience the "Breadcrumb Trail," which she shares with us below.

---

## THE BREADCRUMB TRAIL
### by **Evaleen Whelton**

People often ask, "What led to your diagnosis at thirty-seven?" My internal response is always "The thirty-seven years that went before it!" And that's quite literally the only answer I can give, and then I explain how it's pretty impossible for me to summarize my entire life into a few short sentences. But if I have to summarize, I call it the "Breadcrumb Trail" because that's what it looks like in my very visual mind. The clues to who I really am were laid out in my mind just like the breadcrumbs that Hansel left out so that he and Gretel could find their way home.

Breadcrumbs were little particles of memory that stood out in my mind, like unsolved mysteries or pieces of a story yet to be told. Like the time I was scolded for saying what I thought, or the time I felt small and panicky inside because being around people I didn't know felt like the ground was shaking. Like the time I told my nursery school teacher she wasn't the boss of me, like the time I got so overwhelmed because a friend of mine was not okay. Like the many moments of pain caused by fluorescent lighting or rejection by peers. Or the time I installed dimmer switches on every light fitting in my house. Or like the time I locked my true self away because the world had told me she was not acceptable. Or like the time my head got so hot that I couldn't say what I wanted to say at a staff meeting and so I just sat there, the frustration bubbling inside me as I smiled politely instead of giving voice to the true me. Or like the time the outspoken child had grown into a submissive, people-pleasing adult for fear of upsetting anyone with her thoughts.

The path I was following got especially bumpy just before my arrival home. Shielding my true self and keeping her locked away became increasingly difficult when I became a mom. The constant fear of being seen and being hurt again led to more anxiety. It was around this time that those breadcrumbs came back into my mind and I started to read about autistic women. There, across many articles, lists, and blogs, my life was laid out before me. "That's me!" I thought as my eyes devoured everything they could.

And then the breadcrumbs suddenly changed into light bulbs and my mind literally lit up with "that's why" moments of clarity. Each light fusing with the next, making all those connections over thirty-seven years of not knowing, of not understanding, and of berating myself for not being enough.

At age thirty-seven, all of these breadcrumbs led me home to my community, a beautiful community of people who think like me, feel like me, understand like me, and feel the pulse of the world just like me.

The bright lights settled to a warm glow after the confirmation of my identity on 13th June 2014. It changed my path forever. No longer was I wandering around in the dark with only breadcrumbs to guide me; now I had an illuminated path of understanding, of learning to self love, and of acceptance and pride.

---

Evaleen's experience was quite different from mine. From the very earliest points in my childhood, my mother, who moonlights as my soul mate, noticed that I wasn't quite like my older sister, Emily. It took me longer to walk, even though Emily walked quite early so she wasn't really a good comparison. The differences became more apparent when I was around two years old. Mum noticed I liked things done a certain way and when I decided on a specific task, which was usually lining my toy cars up on my windowsill, it was extremely difficult, if not impossible, to separate me from the activity. These traits continued to become more obvious and my parents had no explanation for my behavior. Awareness of autism wasn't really a thing back then.

My mother took me to see a general practitioner, like any parent would when they were concerned about their child. As is the case with many parents of autistic children, she was saddened by the doctor's determination that the causes for my quirks were either "bad diet" or "inconsistent parenting." At that time the medical community commonly promoted the idea that the parents or some external source almost always caused any developmental difference. Unfortunately, I hear from parents all the time who tell me that this attitude still exists in today's global society, which is frustrating and a very sad thing for everyone involved.

Regarding any child's disability or difference, the debate among professionals and parents is always a heated one. I know this as I have had the personal experience of sitting on both sides of the table: first as an autistic child and now as a social worker. In the course of my work, I've been able to recognize children or young adults who are like me, and I have seen other cases where inconsistencies in home life and communication were most likely the cause of the challenging situation between the parents and child. As a professional, I can see why this is very difficult to determine, but with my autistic edge, I know when other people are like me. I always say, "Fill a room with a thousand people and two autistic people will always find each other."

In any case, Mum persevered when many parents would have been discouraged. Mum would always say that feeling judged by medical professionals was much more emotionally painful for her than any challenge I presented her with when I was very small. This is a common theme between the autistic community and their caregivers, who are often made to feel a sense of inadequacy. The diagnostic process is very challenging for everyone involved.

## I Believe My Child Is Autistic. What Now?

The first step that every autistic person or parent takes is to consult with their doctor. This can be somewhat of a lottery because the response will either be caring and compassionate or judgmental and upsetting. While listening to audiences and answering their questions, I have heard so many experiences that demonstrate this point. There doesn't seem to be a gray area between those two responses. It almost always seems to be one or the other.

I have met with and spoken to autistic groups around the world, both in person and virtually. The question I am asked all the time is,

"My child is autistic. What now?" There is not a single correct answer. Every person is different and every area of the world views autism differently. Add to that the financial and insurance aspects of autism and the waters can get very murky. There isn't a worldwide, uniform global healthcare system. Here in the United Kingdom and Ireland we have the National Health Service (NHS). In most other countries, there is an insurance-based healthcare system. Both seem to have their advantages and disadvantages regarding autism. As the NHS is a public service that is free for all individuals, those who are most in need are prioritized and the waiting lists can be quite long. In a privatized system, waiting lists are not as long, although some people without insurance can be denied services or support when it's required.

Finding similarities in differing healthcare systems isn't always easy, but there is one. The singular thing that was glaringly obvious to everyone I spoke with was that there are long waiting lists for autism support no matter where on the planet one resides. In the US and UK, waiting lists vary depending on the state or local authority and, unfortunately, that time span can range from six months to two years! Parents want to understand their autistic children better, and autistic children and adults want to understand themselves better. Waiting such a long time without a sense of direction can have a profound effect, raising stress levels for all concerned.

The following is a snapshot of what many parents and autistic people face: an initial consultation is done with a general practitioner, a letter is then sent on to psychologists and psychiatrists, and then the waiting game to be offered an appointment begins. Some in the community have told me that the wait time for the initial appointment can be as long as two years. In clinical terms, there isn't much you can do until the appointment letter arrives. In emotional terms, the period between diagnosis and the appointment with the specialist leaves one suscepti-ble, wondering and worrying. The question that is always on one's mind is, "What should I do next?"

I have also learned from speaking with autistic people and parents that they have encountered some level of dishonesty in some clinics because the more treatment is offered the more the clinic receives in revenues. That is rare, but it has happened.

Then, there are some parents who are desperate for help and support of any type. Any "help" that is offered will be agreed to almost instantly because the caregiver is not familiar with autism. They are not concerned with how it might impact their insurance plan or wallet, but are solely focused on how to help their child and are willing to try anything. Families are offered different support therapies, many of which are viewed by the autistic community as extremely controversial. I urge all parents and autistic people to always consider the options that you are offered. Do your own research and seek many opinions. Find out what is available, find out who is providing the service, and have multiple options. Most doctors and therapists have the best interests of their patients at heart. I can't stress strongly enough how important it is to take your time to find the right fit for you and your circumstances. After all, autism is a lifelong experience.

## Research and Learn without Limitation

When I meet with parental groups, and autistic teen or adult groups, I ask questions of the audience, as well as taking questions from them. I always ask those present to raise their hand if they believed early in their child's life that their child was autistic. Of course, given my audience, there is always an ocean of hands raised. I then ask everyone present if there is anyone who was wrong in this belief. I have never encountered a parent or autistic person who thought their children or themselves to be autistic and been wrong in their personal diagnosis.

Parents reach out from around the globe to ask what steps they should take when they see some of the subtle differences like my mother noticed when I was a child. Being able to compare one child to another was helpful for her but in many cases, there is only one child and the parents may not realize that their child is acting differently than other children. As I have stated, the spectrum is vast. Characteristics in autistic children can be rather subtle and may not fully manifest until the child begins to have more interactions with their peers. However, even in the early stages of development, the parents almost always recognize that their child does or reacts to things differently, which prompts the need for a medical diagnosis.

But, sometimes, a medical diagnosis doesn't take place until a child grows to adulthood. A lot of adults read information online, which may spark a "light bulb" moment when they recognize that they may be autistic. Adults that believe they may be autistic ask the same question as parents: "What can I do that will have a positive effect?"

I wish I had a patented answer I could give them. Coming up with a perfect, positive solution that would fit most every person and situation is impossible because the answers to that question must be as uniquely individual as I am.

What if I were to tell you that there are steps that can be taken instantly? The first step is to research autism and autistic people. Learn as much as you can. When I started to research further into autism, the majority of what I found was the disparaging characteristics attributed to autistic people. Other people's words told me that I had a "severe disorder," that I had "communication" difficulties, that I was a "loner," and so on. There are so many negative descriptions that come up via internet search engines when one simply seeks to understand autism.

All of these indictments are negative and can bring an overwhelming sense of fear for parents and for autistics themselves. It all depends on the lens through which one views autism.

Find the lens that is positive. There are wonderful success stories told by autistic people. Listen to them and read about them.

When I was young, there wasn't the ease and luxury of the internet. My parents were left with very demeaning textbooks that only seemed to outline the deficits that the medical community believed I may have. Because of the adverse literature surrounding autism, I felt I was inferior to everyone else and believed that I didn't or couldn't possibly have any gifts that would or could change the world. Many feel doomed to an existence where they believe they are a burden on others. I certainly felt that way. Far too many of my community and peers have expressed that they, too, have felt that weight.

There is not enough literature out there to show that autistic people can grow to live happy and independent lives. Many of us have worked hard to defy the odds placed on us and gain our voices. I use every possible opportunity to urge autistics to tell their story because you never know who will be inspired by it. The primary thing you have to learn is that autistic people are simply different. They are not "normal" people with a "deficit." You or your child are not broken versions of "normal." I urge you never to forget that.

## How to Inspire Yourself and/or Your Child

Everyone's experience of being autistic is uniquely different but one thing remains uniform: there are success stories to be found, if you look.

Until recently, I didn't know that some of the most influential people who have lived are considered by many to have been autistic. A few of those recognizable names are Einstein, Mozart, and Michelangelo. I was a youngster with a vibrant imagination and it would have meant the world to me to have that information. Their passions and desires changed the world forever. I believe that if you look hard enough, you can find an autistic person somewhere in the midst of all that has been good in human history. Personally, I'm sure that it was a passionate and driven autistic Neanderthal who smashed rocks together to create the first spark that made a fire!

There are many autistic heroes you can point out to your autistic child who will certainly inspire them. Some who have been officially diagnosed on the spectrum are actors Sir Anthony Hopkins and Dan Aykroyd, singer Susan Boyle, and economics professor Dr. Vernon Smith. Then there are those who identify as being on the spectrum, like three-time Oscar winner Woody Allen and comedian Jerry Seinfeld. In my opinion, presenting diversely successful role models is a much better strategy than telling them all the faulty things that others have deemed wrong with them. Instilling and developing a sense of pride in the fact that they are an autistic person will help them all through life. To be in the same elite club as the people I listed is a huge honor!

Reading about the creative and upbeat people who were almost certainly autistic will definitely provide some inspiration. You or your child, no matter your gender, can make a difference in this world. If you are among the small minority who believed yourself or your child to be autistic and were wrong in the opinion, you, too, will experience a sense of positivity through autism, as well as a new sense of appreciation. How? By educating yourself about the true nature of autism and the gifts it can bring. With that approach, nobody leaves empty-handed. As an autistic child, I knew I wasn't like my peers, but had I seen all of these epic people, it certainly would have instilled a sense of pride and determination in me from an early age.

## Voluntary and Charitable Autism Groups

The vast majority of groups I meet with are charitable or voluntary groups. Many are run by and for autistic people and their parents, and also for the wider community. Groups like these didn't exist in my youth. My parents didn't have groups like this to reach out to for information or organizations that they could enroll me in to better myself. Today they do exist. Many parents of autistic children and autistics themselves, benefit from this valuable support that is more available now.

Before addressing an organization, I always ask the group manager the same question: "Do you require a diagnosis to join this group?"

The answer to that question has always been a definite "No."

A medical diagnosis can take such a long time to obtain, and groups such as these exist so that some of that gap in time can be filled between the initial consultations and diagnosis day. According to the groups I have met, waiting lists are a universal issue. Because so many people are waiting for one thing or another, I, like others in my community, have learned to communicate over the internet. Online talks came into style very quickly, and I learned that virtual talks followed by "question and answer" sessions were almost as good as an in-person discussion. During the online call or video chat I still asked the same question: "Do you need a diagnosis to join this group?" Their answer, like most others', was an emphatic "No." I find it refreshing that I have never met a support group for parents, children, or adults that needed a confirmed diagnosis in order to join. All of them act under a principle of good faith and understanding, which is welcoming to everyone.

Social media is a very powerful tool for connectivity. No matter where you are, you can look up voluntary or charitable autism causes near you. There are so many to select from that it may require some trial and error before you find a group you think will suit you best. The opportunity to have a conversation with local groups has an amazing effect for all concerned. For autistic children, it gives them a chance to meet with other children like them. Developmental psychologists uniformly agree that it is important for all children to feel connected; this is true for autistic children, too. Growing up, I felt quite alone because I didn't understand the actions of my peers and I didn't know anyone else like me. I didn't understand why or how I was different, but it would have made a huge difference to me had I known that I wasn't the only person out there like me.

I can only imagine what it would have been like to be part of a group that put on activities that are autism friendly. An example is that in today's world, there are many autism-friendly film screenings that give groups like these the opportunity to see movies in cinemas that might otherwise be overwhelming. A sensory-friendly film screening generally consists of less advertising, lower volume, and a reduction of flashing lights. I am a huge fan of autism-friendly screenings! Screenings like this are open to the public and often invite groups to come to the theater.

Children's movies tend to have a lot of flashing lights and annoying, blaring music, which means I can't enjoy them without additional stress. When my son, Ethan, wants to see a new release, I look for the autism screening. I do this not because of Ethan, but for me. Ethan isn't like me; he is not autistic. This makes it nice for us because, even though we exist in two different universes, he lets me into his and, from time to time, I can allow him into mine. What I teach Ethan is that my universe is different. It is not a deficient version of his; it is just different, and both are to be respected. I need to give him a few more years to understand, though, because as I write this he is still young and doesn't grasp all the intricacies of my world.

As a small child I went to a mixed-abilities playgroup and I thrived. Although my intellect was always high, I was difficult to understand and I was very mistrusting of everyone who wasn't one of my parents. The reason I did so well at the playground was because some of the other children were like me. We autistics seem to have an unspoken understanding between one another. We all know the score.

Sometimes I wonder what my life would have been like if I had been more active in a group that associated with more autistic people. My childhood situation wasn't remarkable or too different from anybody else's. I spent most of my time at home with my mum while my dad went to work and Emily went to school. I don't recall a lot of my childhood other than the constant mental assessment of why other people thought what I was doing was wrong or somehow upsetting to them. In my mind, lining up my toy cars and wearing my Superman costume twenty-four hours a day were essential for the world to remain firmly on its axis. At some point, I'm sure I probably thought, "Why isn't Mum dressed as Superman, too? Strange lady!"

There are autism advocates who criticize parents of autistic children for openly discussing what they find difficult in the upbringing of their autistic child or children. I don't agree with this premise. My mum wasn't deeply knowledgeable about autism when I was a child. She felt that the reason I wasn't doing things the way other children did was her fault. I didn't sleep well as a child and was always awake very early. I liked all my days to be the same when I was young; I didn't understand that deviations in patterns are important for flexibility in life. For all human beings, not just autistics, eating and drinking fluids is a must and in order to achieve this, grocery shopping must be done. I couldn't stay at home by myself, so I had to come along for the ordeal—and I do not use that term lightly. It was an ordeal for both Mum and me and, as a grown man, I still detest grocery shopping. I didn't know how to communicate my feelings and my mum didn't know how to deal with all this. She didn't have anyone to reach out to for support and knowledge. After all, I was still on a waiting list for further assessment.

Autism support groups also help parents. They provide parents the chance to meet other parents who are in the same position. Sometimes there are expectations from the autistic community that everyone does know or should know all there is to know about autism. That just isn't the case, especially for young parents with no prior experience with autism. Mum lived a lonely existence and freely admits that she wasn't always able to communicate in a way that made sense to me. Likewise, I couldn't always make my feelings or wishes known to her. I finally understood a small piece of what she went through after Ethan was born and developed colic. When he cried early in the morning, Mum laughed at the karma that had befallen me.

Support groups also welcome non-autistic siblings, too! I wouldn't have thought that was an option, as I believed such a group would only be for autistic children and their parents. But I learned I was wrong and the siblings are a wonderful addition. I've now visited several groups where non-autistic siblings were present and it was very heartwarming to experience. The contributions that are made are inspiring. In every way, the interaction makes perfect sense.

I related to their experiences together because there were two vastly different children growing up in our household: Emily, who is not autistic, and me. Emily was my first friend and was able to understand me before any other children my age could. When I became terribly upset at school, my teacher and classroom assistant would send for her so that we could go for a walk together until I felt okay again. I still enjoy the comfort of familiar faces, especially those I care about. I loved being around Emily, as she knew what I was like and I knew she would look out for me. She still does to this day.

One of the first groups I visited was a group close to where I live in Derry. This was my first experience meeting with an autism group and I was very keen to see what it was like. I felt right at home! Even though the group had young children, they knew I was like them. I loved seeing all the children playing together and parents being able to have a cup of tea and chat. It was my first experience and it was quite overwhelming. The children were enjoying themselves and I even spoke with some of them about their special interests. Of course, my passion for all things *Titanic* came out in full geek mode when one of the children was wearing a *Titanic* T-shirt. The little boy told me that he knew everything about the *Titanic* and I excitedly responded that I did, too. He told me to ask him any question about the ship and her construction. I immediately went through my mental filing cabinet to find the most obscure fact. I smugly asked the seven- or eight-year-old boy how many toilets there were on the ship. He smiled proudly and said, "Two hundred seventy-five toilets." He was right and I was speechless!

Many of the parents present wanted to ask me questions about my first book, *Why Does Daddy Always Look So Sad?*, and how my mum coped with me in certain situations that weren't mentioned in the book. They wanted to know how she managed with things such as trips to the dentist, sitting in traffic, and finding an exact replacement for a broken toy. The only answer I could give was, "With great dignity," because there was no one around to consult with, so she had to devise her own ways of getting me through such processes.

I found it comforting that all the parents in attendance shared a similar message; they felt lost but, when they found the group, their spirits lifted immensely and the kids had the opportunity to meet other kids like them. Many parents reported that their mental health dramatically improved because their children were happy and no longer felt alone in the world. I think that was true for the parents, too. Some of the children were very inquisitive and asked me questions. I answered every question but if I didn't know an answer, I told them so. I love seeing the kids actively involved in interacting, in their own ways, in these discussions. When they are comfortable, they are little question machines. By the end of the event I find myself wishing that I had had an adult like me to ask questions of when I was young.

Autistic children know they aren't like the others in their classrooms, too. Children are acutely aware of the negative stereotypes that autism brings, even from an early age. One little girl asked me, "Why does everyone ask me to look at them when they are talking?"

This was hard for me to hear, as children are still encouraged, and sometimes even forced, to make eye contact, even though it is so far out of their comfort zone. I told her that she didn't have to if she didn't want to, which was a revelation for her.

Another time I was explaining that I grew up to become a social worker and that I worked with vulnerable children and adults. A young boy raised his hand and asked, "As a social worker, are you like the dog warden, but . . . for people?" The hall erupted with laughter; we all understood the humor. The old saying is true: children do say the funniest things.

There are groups that also have set days for adult meetings. I have attended several and discovered that many adults were diagnosed later in life. Most said that when they received their diagnosis, or at least while they were waiting for it, they felt a sense of relief. They finally had an explanation for why they felt dissimilar to most everyone else. Many in the group were middle-aged and married, and they came from a variety of career paths. Like the kids, they felt a sense of comfort while they were around others who were like them. Several said that their spouses felt a similar relief because they finally had reasons why their significant other was different. Some said this insight and what they had learned from the group and the advice they were given saved their marriage! I was fascinated to learn that knowing that one partner was autistic changed communication within the relationship and that alone had helped strengthen their bond.

Participating in autism awareness groups such as these can be invaluable for both the families and the autistic individuals. The numerous charitable associations that advocate for people with autism spread awareness and knowledge about autism that generally helps individuals and family members recognize the many ways we autistic people can excel. They can help us understand ourselves better because they promote sharing experiences of both the autistic individual and their family members. The majority of the organizations support the idea that autistic people should no longer be collectively stigmatized or viewed as a burden, but should be allowed to flourish as individuals and members of society.

Leanne Lewis has lived a very unique experience because her children, as well as she and her husband, are part of the spectrum, even though they were not aware of that at the time of their son's diagnosis. Her story, below, provides valuable insight on awareness and understanding, and how they can blossom into a more comfortable and supportive life for autistic people.

---

## HOW A POSITIVE SPIN ON DIAGNOSIS AND DISCLOSING CAN BENEFIT OTHER PARENTS
*by* **Leanne Lewis**

We knew that our son was autistic long before he was officially diagnosed. He used to spin in the goal instead of taking part in football training; during the school play he was on the stage spinning, vocalizing, and covering his ears, while his peers were happily singing and dancing. It beggars belief that the school completely missed his autism. As so often happens, all of the incidents and issues at school (of which there were many) were put down to "behavioral issues" and his "lack of focus."

We moved our son to a different school which, thankfully, recognized and supported his needs straightaway. However, there was one battle that we still had on our hands: getting an official diagnosis, which was the only way he would be granted official SNA (special needs assistant) access.

The diagnostic procedure can be long and arduous. It took over a year of gentle (and not-so-gentle!) persistence to go through the entire process. It can take years for children to even begin the assessment process, so we were lucky compared to some, or perhaps they just wanted to be rid of me. My one piece of advice to parents trying to get their children assessed is to be persistent. Know your rights and don't settle for anything less!

We started the slow and gentle process of disclosure during the assessment period.

We started by explaining to him about difference, not related to autism at all. Basically, no two people are the same. Everyone is different and that is okay. People have different hair color, eye color, abilities, and interests. Wouldn't the world be a boring place if everyone was the same?

We then started to explain differences in terms of individual sensory experiences of the world. Not only do people look different and have different abilities and interests, but they also see, hear, and smell things differently. Being a late-diagnosed autistic adult, I really wish that someone had taught this to me as a child; it would have explained so much.

We explained about sensory differences in context. For example, he is hypersensitive to sound, so if we felt that he was struggling with a noisy setting, we would explain about how people experience sound differently. Some people wouldn't even notice noises; other people would hear them but not loudly, whereas for others the sound would be unbearable, and even painful. In terms of sensory differences, we are all different and that is okay!

We taught him that we need to learn to predict when we may find a situation difficult or recognize when we are struggling and do something about it to prevent it or make it easier. For example, in a noisy environment we could wear ear defenders, reduce the noise in the environment, or move to a quieter place.

He is also hypersensitive to light, which happens to be my own main sensory issue. If it was too bright, then we would explain that different people have different sensitivities to light and that to him light can sometimes be too much. We also taught him that we could do things to help with that: wearing glasses, shutting blinds, or turning off lights. Everyone has different experiences of light, and guess what, that is okay!

We also made sure we pointed out differences related to his strengths. The dialogue surrounding autism can be extremely negative, with the sole focus being on "deficits." We feel that it is just as important, maybe even more so, to point out and focus on his wonderful strengths, of which there are so many.

Our son never questioned why he went to so many appointments, and we chose not to explain the reason to him at that point. He wasn't worried about the appointments and we didn't want him to question whether there was anything wrong with him. After all, there wasn't. He is just different, not broken. If he had asked, then we would have explained it to him in as gentle a way as possible.

We didn't disclose his diagnosis to him straightaway. Even though we knew he was autistic and were fine with it, there was still a huge surge of emotion on receiving the diagnosis. The process had been long and stressful to us as parents, but not to him, thankfully. The most predominant emotion we experienced was relief. Relief that we didn't have to fight any more to get the right experts to assess him, that they had seen what we already knew, and that he would now qualify for the support he needed at school.

In terms of disclosing his autism diagnosis, the groundwork had already been done before he received his official diagnosis. He understood that everyone is different in terms of appearance, likes, dislikes, strengths, and sensory experiences of the world. The next step was to help him understand that everyone also has different brains. Not better, not worse, just different. Everyone has different brains, and you know what, that is okay!

We never had an official sit-down chat disclosing his autism. Again, it was very gentle and at a time that he was happy and relaxed. It was within a couple of weeks of us receiving his diagnosis. The time just felt right. We explained that everyone has different brains, and that in our family ours happen to be autistic brains. It really wasn't an issue at all. In fact, he said okay and started talking about his "special interest." Gradually over time we started dropping the word autism into conversations.

Previously, we explained that he was finding a setting or activity too noisy because he experiences sound differently, as does everyone. Now we explained that autistics often experience sound differently: some autistics are hyposensitive to sound, some autistics are hypersensitive to sound (like us), and other autistics are not bothered by it at all.

Disclosure for us wasn't a big deal. I suspect that it helped that his brothers also received their diagnoses within a short time frame. All three boys went through the assessment process simultaneously and were diagnosed within a three-month period.

During the assessment process, my husband and I had both come to the realization that we are also autistic. I think that also helped, as we could talk to the boys about our own autistic experiences. It is completely normal to be autistic in our household, as we all are. We know nothing different.

The diagnostic process is inherently negative due to autism being diagnosed based on deficits listed in the *DSM-5* (*Diagnostic and Statistical Manual of Mental Disorders*, fifth edition). We had fantastic diagnostic teams, but the process left me feeling drained. After the diagnosis, I needed to shift my thinking from all the deficits that were focused on during the diagnostic procedure toward looking at the amazing positives that we all have, which, sadly, were somewhat irrelevant during the diagnostic process.

I started painting positive traits of autism on rocks, partly to help shift my lens, but also to help my children see that there are so many positive attributes they possess. There are too many to list here, but I'd say some of their main attributes are their intelligence, honesty, humor, kindness, empathy (we experience hyper-empathy), and ability to think outside the box. They are unique individuals and are amazing in their own right; so much more than the list of deficits outlined in the *DSM-5*. They need to grow up surrounded by messages of positivity about themselves

and autism, which will hopefully counteract the negative perceptions and prejudice they will encounter in society.

My children are aware of their challenges; they need to be
so they can learn to manage them and self-advocate for their
own needs. However, we try to focus more on their amazing
strengths. They get involved with painting autism stones and
plant them around the local community, to also help shift society's perspective and dialogue on autism. We established The
Autism Stone Challenge embracing autism campaign to encourage others to do the same.

Telling our children about autistic role models and reading
them books by autistic children has also helped them to see
autism in a positive light.

Our children accepted their diagnoses easily and without question, probably due to the long, gentle, and positive
approach we took. They are now being taught to self-advocate,
so that they grow up with the confidence to advocate for themselves, each other, and fellow autistics.

---

The diagnostic process can be emotionally painful and mentally frustrating, or it can be empowering, as Leanne demonstrates in her story
and her life. If you think you are autistic, or someone close to you is
autistic, don't retreat from life. Instead, once you recognize that there
are differences that may indicate autism, explore programs that are
immediately available, even if you have to wait for a medical diagnosis. Reinforce the positive aspects of life and recognize the possibilities
that await each individual.

# 4

# Should I Tell My Child
# They Are Autistic?

When children and adults are diagnosed autistic, there can be some bumps in the road when it comes to having *that* conversation. How do you tell them of their diagnosis? A lot of parents can, at last, breathe a sigh of relief because they finally have an answer as to why their child or loved one is different. In truth, a diagnosis should only serve one purpose: to inform people about something that they already know, or at least suspect, about their loved ones.

When children are told that they are autistic, they have different reactions. Some can feel a sense of belonging, especially when they understand that there are many other children out there just like them. Even when I see children at autism events or settings, the little community that is forged is incredibly endearing. Everyone has their own little purpose, working together without judgment. Even as a grown man, I feel at home with them because they are like me and because of that recognition, I have often been delegated tasks or assignments by the young group members.

When children know they are autistic and are informed that it is fine for them to be proud to be so, the seeds for self-advocacy are planted early on in their lives. The sense of difference and distance between them and the rest of the world diminishes.

Like all children, when they are free to voice their opinions and wishes, they flourish. They learn how to communicate better with people around them. Sadly, many autistic children go into therapies that only teach the skill of telling people what they want to hear or regurgitating what has been drilled into them. Those children usually end up limiting themselves by doing what they feel is expected of them.

Everyone needs to understand that having a label like "autism" automatically generates feelings of self-inadequacy and denial because we don't think we can fit into the outside world. I know this firsthand; this was me. It is not easy feeling like you are diseased or have less worth or capabilities than those who are not autistic. This is how I viewed myself when I was younger. There weren't enough positive and empowering voices available to reinforce my self-esteem. I didn't tell anyone I was autistic, even after I knew. Reflecting on this now, I understand that I tried to hide who I was because I felt that I would be judged or lose respect from people I cared about.

In societal terms, there is a huge difference when telling someone of a medical diagnosis versus a psychiatric diagnosis. This doesn't just apply to autism but also to a mental health diagnosis. Many parents have said that they would find it easier to tell their child that they had serious underlying physical health problem like epilepsy or asthma than to tell them they had autism or a mental health issue. Why would they feel that way? The short answer is stigma. I would love to report that in the twenty-first century, the world has developed into an accepting, progressive place. In truth, it hasn't. If there weren't a stigma around autism, this book wouldn't have been written.

Like anything in life, disclosing and discussing a difficult topic comes down to one key factor: approach. There certainly isn't a one-size-fits-all approach to telling people that they are autistic. I would be the first to say that I wouldn't have handled my diagnosis very well when I was a child or in my early teens. It would have been much harder for my parents to apply a positive approach, because there wasn't a lot of positive and meaningful literature for parents back then and there weren't any autistic heroes they could use to reinforce a sense of equity. Too much of the available data was the medical-model negativity of the time.

Whenever I finish telling my own story onstage, I invite questions from all attendees. I never leave until everyone who wants to ask me something has done so, and I will always take time to meet people who want to ask me something privately. Many bring their children with them and I love that. I have designed my talks, seminars, and training courses in such a way to reassure and inspire autistic people and non-autistic people that not only is being different okay, but also it's a blessing.

One of the questions I'm asked most is, "Should I tell my child?" Matthew is a young man I met at one of my conferences who grew up not knowing, or understanding, what made him different. As we spoke about his passion for dinosaurs and feeling empathy toward others, he revealed how he learned he was autistic.

## The Boy Who Wasn't Told

Matthew loves dinosaurs. He is now nineteen and was formally diagnosed autistic when he was four years old. He can name every single species of dinosaur and tell you exactly what their preferred meals were. All one must do is give Matthew a species of dinosaur and he will reply if they were herbivorous, carnivorous, or omnivorous. He and I had delightful conversations about the extinct creatures but, no matter how hard I tried, I couldn't stump the young man. He was an encyclopedia on the subject!

Matthew always wondered why people didn't share his deep love of dinosaurs. He told me that as a small child he had a dinosaur figure that he would carry with him everywhere. It was a velociraptor figure and it was the only one small enough to fit in his pocket comfortably. He would pull the small figure from his pocket and explain it to other children on the playground, but they walked away from him and didn't want to discuss it.

This left Matthew in tears, as he couldn't possibly understand why other children didn't share his deep love of the late Jurassic period of our history. Matthew often asked his parents why nobody else loved dinosaurs or liked him talking about them. His parents told him that nobody else's opinion mattered and if it was his love and passion then he should not be deterred. Because he was young, they didn't want to tell him he was autistic, which meant he was different than some of the other children.

Eventually, Matthew was told when he was sixteen and he admits that he immediately felt anger that he didn't know this sooner in his life. Matthew knew he was different; he had always known. Yet, no one explained what made him different. When he asked his parents why they hadn't told him, they gave him a common answer: they didn't like the idea of their child being labeled. Today Matthew feels no ill will toward his parents for not telling him sooner that he is autistic.

I cannot stress enough the stigma that autism blankets us in. When Matthew was growing up and in this present day, there is much more stigma attached to autism without much understanding of what it means to each of us. Matthew had to endure the same sadness caused by hurtful stereotypes imposed upon him. He carries the same unseen, but painful, scars most of us have buried inside us.

I can relate to Matthew's story in many ways. My mother didn't tell me until I was nineteen; by then I was on the cusp of beginning my social work training. Parents do not wish to have labels placed on their children, and I totally understand that. One of those "labels" that Matthew and I discussed at length was the notion that someone with autism lacks empathy. It's often called an "autistic trait" and it makes me shudder whenever I hear it or read it. While Matthew and I spoke about empathy, I was able to truly empathize with Matthew as I had been in his position, living life asking why I am the way I am. Being able to absorb your surroundings and wonder where your place is within that world is only truly understood by those who have experienced it.

I was the same in that, with the eyes of maturity, I didn't resent or blame my parents for not telling me sooner in life. All children want to fit in and find a sense of belonging. Every human being needs that as a foundation to build upon. There are some parents who feel that the negative connotations attached to the word "autism" are too easily discoverable and may upset the children who find them. I understand that as I had access to the internet, despite it being rather primitive compared to what it is now. I easily navigated to sites where I saw the horrible and unhelpful stereotypes. The one that Matthew was labeled with is "obsessive and repetitive behaviors."

Mainstream services, well-known charities, and groups that discuss autism often analyze this "distressing symptom or trait." My heart tends to get heavy with sorrow when I imagine autistic children or teenagers reading about themselves on these "supportive" websites. In my mind I can see them pulling back and deciding their love of whatever they are passionate about must stop. Had I read these websites at a younger age, I would have put my toy cars back in the boxes. Matthew would have lost his love for dinosaurs. No child should ever have to feel guilty about what they love, no matter how insignificant or tedious it may seem to others.

When autistic children line up cars or show everyone their toy dinosaur, who decides that this is inappropriate? Just because a child plays in a specific way, or finds amusement or contentment in a repetitive motion, doesn't mean that that way of interacting with toys and gadgets is wrong. I used to wonder if there was a committee of people who decided when an individual was doing something differently and if it should be stopped. I wondered who and what defined different. And why do people want to cure it? Is there anything wrong with being different if it isn't harmful? It is something that, even today, I don't fully understand. Maybe autistic people are much more tolerant by default.

## The Autistic Superhero

I don't always have an answer for every single person who asks me a question. Regrettably, I am only human and don't know how to provide a tailor-made answer for each individual question. One of my favorite parts about speaking is interacting with audiences and hearing what they have to say. I think it is important, as I want to learn from other people's experiences, too. I only know of one experience: my own. So, when someone tells me their story that is uplifting, I appreciate it and retain it because I know it can help others down the road.

This is one of those special stories. It's a wonderful description about how parents told their daughter that she is autistic. They explained it to her like it was a gift.

Sophie always found that her schoolwork wasn't challenging enough for her. She always had her work done first, pencil case organized, and often preferred to do tasks by herself rather than with other people. Pupils in her class teased her for having her work done so quickly, to the point where she deliberately tried to slow down to match the speed of everyone else.

Sophie was eight years old when she was diagnosed and was always incredibly lucky to have supportive teachers and close friends. Sophie asked her parents the same question I asked mine: "Why am I not like the others in my class?"

Sophie's parents knew immediately that there is a huge stigma surrounding autism and there are many derogatory and unflattering terms that are used to define us. Like every parent, they didn't want her to be encumbered by a negative perception of herself, especially at such a young age. Sophie loved superheroes when she was small. Her parents employed that love of superheroes and told her that she had special powers of her own because she was autistic. They explained that her brain and mind were different from everybody else's and that would help her in life and not hold her back.

Sophie wanted to know if she could fly, see through walls, and melt steel beams with her eyes. Rather than her parents denying it, they said that one day she could! Sophie was always proficient with numbers and loved researching the cosmos and all things physics. Sophie's parents give us a fine example of a strengths-based approach. Their technique immediately boosted Sophie's confidence and celebrated her difference. She loved the idea of being a superhero. She told all her classmates that she had superpowers, so much so that everyone else wanted them, too.

Sophie has always been proud of who she is. It was instilled in her from a very young age. Sophie started university this year and will be studying atomic physics with a goal of becoming a global leader in that field. I have no doubt that she will.

Sophie has traveled around Europe and the Americas meeting people like her and being a proud member of the autistic community. When Sophie came home from her travels, her mother said to her, "Remember? I told you that you could fly! I was telling the truth."

The people in Sophie's life had always nurtured her love, passion, and skill for understanding the building blocks of atomic reality. When I spoke with her, I was thrilled to hear her say that she has always been proud of who she is.

I told her that I wasn't always proud of myself, that I tried to hide being different and that I felt like I needed major repair compared to my "normal peers." Sophie couldn't understand this! She had been instilled with such pride in herself from the very beginning. It was incredibly heartwarming and an attitude I wish I had grown up with. This isn't my parents' fault; the fault lies with me. I was emotionally intelligent enough to know I was different, but I made the conscious decision not to accept it.

## The Positive Approach

It took me many years to accept and love myself for who I am. I constantly hid and masked who I was because I wanted to be accepted by those around me. Many autistic people can empathize with this because so many have also felt that they had to do it over the years. For years, we always felt like we needed to have the approval of others or a special invitation to join in with the crowd. One of my goals in life is to contribute toward no child or adult having to hide who they are.

I believe the majority of children probably care deeply about what others think of them as an automatic response. What if that was to change? What if they could confidently say they are autistic and that was fine with their peers? There shouldn't be so much emphasis on fitting in, but rather celebration for someone who stands out. It actually benefits all children. I know that is amazingly easy for me to say as a grown man, but surely we can change the narratives at some point? At school, I did everything I could to try and fit in. If I had known how to celebrate my own differences, never mind anyone else celebrating them on my behalf, I likely would have tried less and been myself more.

With a huge injection of positivity, I probably would have had a much happier existence in my youth. There are a growing number of autistic voices that want to inspire and motivate people, myself included. If you always steer the ships in a positive direction, as autistic children grow, the talents and gifts they have to share with the world will humble you.

## Parental Feelings

Parents have confided to me a variety of reactions when it comes to their children being different, whether they were told via diagnosis or realized it for themselves. When children are struggling, it triggers pessimistic responses. Most parents are protective of their children, even me. If Ethan gets up to mischief at school, it reminds me of some of the memories I have from when I was at school. Ethan isn't autistic, but even when Ethan has a little misdemeanor I admit that I can become protective of him. Oddly, it's almost like an immediate bias that I have, based on what I experienced as a child.

Something I have learned that I find incredible is that many parents have been diagnosed autistic after their child has been diagnosed! Through children, some adults discover that they are different, too, or that they live their lives very much in the same manner as their children do.

Numerous parents go to psychologists or undergo some form of counseling before telling their children they are autistic in order to remove any latent bias toward the topic. The reasoning behind this is because it is important to work through any misgivings prior to having any conversation because autistic children can pick up anxieties and fears that parents may have.

Along that same line of thought, there are parents who do not want to disclose the autism diagnosis to the child, or anyone else, because they are fearful that classmates will mistreat the child. Even though it is rarely intentional, children can be cruel to each other. It's natural that parents become protective when they hear horror stories of children being bullied for being obsessive or awkward. This is a primary reason to promote and teach acceptance of each other's oddities. We all have them. Let's celebrate them instead of condemning them.

Several parents have told me that they are afraid their children won't be able to understand the diagnosis or that they might become more depressed as a result of the conversation. Parents also generally fear that the autism label may discourage their children from exploring positive possibilities about themselves. They also fear that the child might not take advantage of opportunities. My parents had these fears when it came to telling me.

These positions are very valid and understandable. It is certain that one or more of these issues will arise at some point. But, with compassion and a different approach, these can be resolved. Look at the positive approach taken by Sophie's parents. They never let her feel that she was anything less than gifted. She always believed being autistic was an advantage for her. Unfortunately, that wasn't the case for Matthew. I urge everyone to listen to all voices, especially autistic voices that promote acceptance. We are telling you what we need so that we can contribute, too.

No matter what issues come to the surface, with patient and compassionate parenting, they can invariably be resolved. As I said earlier, almost all children strive to fit in with their peers. My non-autistic sister did the same thing and, while we interact with life and nature differently, the common theme of peer acceptance was still prominent with both of us. While she and I have different operating systems inside our minds, the inherent survival instinct to fit in was equally as strong in each of us.

Based on discussions I've had with autistic people, their parents, their teachers, and their siblings, autistic people who progressed into adulthood and were never told that they were autistic lived an awfully long time with frustration and depression. The lingering self-asked question of "Why am I different?" festers over time and, when you don't know the answer, it only builds frustration within those who live every day asking that question. It seems to be a major contributing factor to mental health problems incurred by a significant percentage of autistic people.

If parents choose not to tell their autistic child the reason for their differences, they will probably find out later in life and spend many painfully confused hours trying to figure out why they are different. This approach is much less common now than what it was in the past, but there is still a minority out there that will not disclose.

I had a lot of support when I was young and I never actually questioned the real reason for the assistance or the terminology attached to me, but deep down I knew why I needed them and why they were there. I understood my situation more than people gave me credit for, even though at times I resented it. At thirteen, I probably couldn't have told you what the word "autism" meant, but I certainly could list why things I did were not like others in my classroom or family.

Having additional support systems means that parents can get advice and ideas from other parents who experience similar issues. Sophie's story is very inspiring to everyone, and it provides parents with ideas of how they can positively impact their child as they disclose why their child is different. While optimism may benefit some, everyone is different, and comparing histories of Matthew and Sophie, I can see that both approaches have merit. As a parent, I feel the need to protect my child from any emotional pain or trauma, but I also feel the need to let him excel with positive reinforcement. These decisions are as individual as you or I and require open, heartfelt discussions with an eye to the future of the child.

## Choosing When to Tell Someone about a Diagnosis

Children are being diagnosed much sooner in life than in previous decades. Parents and professionals have a higher level of awareness of all aspects of autism and they have a deeper understanding that there can be positivity attached to it. Parents know their child better than anyone else. One child may have the maturity level and understanding that can receive this information at the age of six. However, at the age of twelve, I probably wouldn't have been able to handle such a conversation with my parents.

Parents have to be emotionally prepared for honest discussions with each other, educators, friends, and family. There will always be a debate whether, and when, it's the right time to have the conversation with the child. Most parents will spend hours in turmoil deciding if and when they should tell their autistic child that they are autistic. There isn't a specific age that a child can or should be told. Parents know their children best and are most capable of gauging whether the child is emotionally ready to have such a discussion. It is, after all, the discretion of each individual parent.

There is another point to consider, too. Children can have terribly negative experiences at school, and being bullied is almost always a feature that autistic people remember and talk about when recalling their education. I am no different. As a student, I quickly reacted to bullying and it often landed me in hot water. At the time, I didn't realize that I was directly contributing to the problem by giving my classmates the reaction they wanted. Telling a child who is already having a difficult time in school and with other students can be detrimental to the child, which is why many parents wait until their child is in a better headspace before having the autism discussion with them.

There is no right or wrong time for this discussion. It has to be predicated on an understanding of the child, their environment, their needs, and the coping mechanisms around them. Obviously, one must consider the child's probable reaction to the discussion but it's also important to think beyond the present moment and into the child's future. How will this discussion affect them now and in the future? The ultimate goal is to do the best for the child.

## How to Explain the Diagnosis to Your Child

I love the idea of emphasizing positives during such a conversation. I would love to travel back to my school days to tell myself of my own diagnosis. I would never highlight why I couldn't sit still for long, why I would line up my toy cars, that I found group tasks challenging, or that when I'm not interested in something, I am difficult to engage. I would never ruin my own self-esteem. Little Jude and adult Jude are as autistic as they ever were or will be. My childhood self was somebody I was always ashamed of before I learned to accept my childhood, heal, and move on.

I would reassure myself that one day I would have a happy and fulfilling life, that why I am who I am will, hopefully, change the world one day. I would ask myself, "Why do you think you are very organized?" or

"Why do you think you read books far beyond what would be considered age-appropriate material?" and other questions like those.

When I am told something, no matter how positive or negative it is, I always take time to digest it. I retreat, write things down, and try to identify gaps in my own understanding of the topic. Later in the day, or even the week, I will come back to the discloser with a long list of questions to clarify things. I have learned from many autistic adults that a lot of us do the same thing. So perhaps be prepared if your child reacts in a similar manner when told of something important like a diagnosis.

As far as a conversation goes, it doesn't always have to be a verbal or spoken conversation. There are more and more books out there that have been written by autistic adults in such a way that they are empowering to small children. There are many visual aids and books that can explain things to small children in a wonderful way that inspires them rather than upsetting them or provoking anger. There are even videos out there that have received tremendous approval from the autistic community to help parents apply positivity in their approaches to the topic.

The most important thing is to be there for your autistic child. If they have a question, do your best to answer it honestly, with compassionate understanding. If you don't have an answer, tell them you don't know but you will do your best to find out. Don't push them for a reaction; let them sort it out in their way. Reinforce that you are there to support them but allow the process they go through to unfold. Respect them, love them, and honor their uniqueness.

## Going Forward after an Autism Diagnosis

There are so many meaningful and wonderful things that being autistic can bring about. Many innovative and wonderful things done by our species have come to fruition from a mind that occupies a place on the spectrum. Just look at the ceiling of the Sistine Chapel in Rome, or listen to Mozart's compositions. While neither of the men was defined as autistic in their lifetimes, many believe they were on the spectrum, and their astute attention to detail certainly seconds that view in my eyes. Showcasing autistic heroes to your children will inspire them, and if your child has a special interest, you can probably find an autistic person somehow involved in the topic. It may take some research but the effort will be worthwhile.

Telling your child autism is nothing to be ashamed of may help the child start their journey of self-acceptance. There is a growing body of information about neurodiversity that teaches that being different is okay. Presenting this to the child will help them relate to the fact that everyone is different and that each of us can excel in life.

Personally, I have a vision in which every child who is different can freely be so; without intimidation, bullying, and fear; without someone trying to fix them; and without good-intentioned people trying to mold them into something they are not. Finally, and most important in my vision, each child is loved and respected for being exactly who they are.

# 5

# Do Vaccines Cause Autism?

I have traveled to many places and met many people. One of the most prevalent questions I am asked is what my position is when it comes to vaccines. I was once told that one of the most important aspects of being a speaker is to be a listener, and I have heard the stories behind why so many hold the belief that vaccines cause children to be autistic. And I have heard the stories that support the other side that believes vaccines have nothing to do with being autistic.

General skepticism of vaccines began back in the 1800s with the release of the smallpox vaccine. It was something new and it was difficult to understand how giving someone a dose of the illness could keep them from getting it. People didn't understand that it was designed to train the immune system so that it recognized the illness and fought against it. Instead they thought it would give them the deadly disease.

Autism has also been attributed to low birth weight. Again, there isn't a wide range of scientific evidence to support that babies with low birth weight tend to be autistic. There have been some theories put forth but none are actually listed anywhere credible. Hypotheses that low birth weight is a contributory factor have not been thoroughly documented.

Today many people believe that the old deadly illnesses like smallpox and measles have been eradicated, but recent outbreaks of measles have shown that isn't true. The vaccinations did what they were designed to do, and as soon as people stopped vaccinating their children for measles, the deadly illness began a comeback in various areas of the world. Some families refuse vaccines because of religious issues, and some just feel that with proper hygiene, they will be safe. There are some people who don't trust pharmaceutical companies and feel the vaccines might cause worse health conditions, like autism.

## What Causes Autism?

There is no definite answer as to what causes autism. The first line of inquiry seems to be genetics. Many families have autistic children and later discover that an uncle or aunt was also autistic, a discovery that is often made in adulthood as diagnoses for children are much simpler today. In the 1980s and early 1990s, autistic children were considered naughty and uncontrollable and didn't like or respect authority. At that time teachers and professionals didn't have the wide range of knowledge on autism that they have today.

As for the genetic discussion, I would have to note that I have a non-autistic son, which indicates that not every autistic person will be the parent of an autistic child. However, I have met many parents who are autistic and now have autistic children themselves. Even with extensive genetic and DNA testing, there has not been a definitive link between chromosomal or genetic abnormalities and a person being autistic.

There have been some links made between autistic children and parents over a certain age. I do not fall into this category, given that my mother was twenty-five when I was born. I did meet one parent who had a baby boy when she was forty-seven. The boy is autistic and, given her age at the time of her son's birth, she feels a sense of guilt. No parent should ever feel guilty or ashamed at having an autistic child. Guilt stands in the way of betterment for both the parent and the child, and we hold enough shame of our own without parents adding to it. There are enough horrible theories that being autistic is a vile negative in life.

I am not saying that being autistic is easy; sometimes I have my own internal struggles, like not knowing what to do if someone I love is distressed or upset. I am not a monster, deprived of empathy or understanding of other people; I just process and deal with information slightly differently from everyone else. I am not ashamed of this anymore. There doesn't seem to be the same stigma for anything else in life, including color-blindness, tone-deafness, or any other difference in sensory processing. It is important to note that autism is *not* an intellectual disability. In the past, the word "autism" was used to describe a person who had an intellectual disability. Many studies have shown that autistic people tend to have normal or above-average intelligence. There are individuals with intellectual disabilities who also happen to be autistic, but autism itself is certainly not a learning disability, as some believe it to be.

The notion that those who have an intellectual disability are "more autistic" than others also needs to end. Severity segregation is a real issue that I have faced myself. The idea that my ability to drive, have a car, grow a thick luscious beard, hold a conversation for over thirty seconds, and parent a child would qualify me as "less autistic" than other people is absurd. It simply isn't the case. The terms "autistic" and "intellectual disability" are not interchangeable. They are very different issues that sometimes cross paths. As repeated very frequently, the main message of this book is that *autism is simply a different way of thinking or being.*

Realistically, there is no real evidence out there to show what causes autism. Is research focused in the wrong direction? Sometimes I think it is. If the same amount of funds were allocated to increase the acceptance and understanding of autism and neurodiversity, many children would not grow up feeling ashamed because they are different from the majority. Maybe, instead of asking *why* autism exists, we should be asking *how* we can learn to accept people who don't process things the same way as everyone else.

## My Final Thoughts

I don't want to focus on a forensic examination of what factors may or may not cause autism. There are numerous links and resources through the CDC and WHO and other research facilities to explore the genetic factors, vaccine controversy, and environmental exposure information. I want to share my experiences and let each of you decide what is best for you and those you care about.

A very common denominator for refusal to vaccinate is the fear of autism. All over the internet, there are figures, statistics, and data that show the rising mortality rates of measles, mumps, and rubella. There are many anti-vax (anti-vaccination) websites and organizations that say vaccinations cause autism.

I wonder if they feel being autistic is worse than dying of measles or some other disease that there is a vaccine for. In many cases, the measles can be mild and a full recovery can be expected. But here is a hypothetical scenario, albeit a realistic one if you live in a country or region that still has clusters of measles cases. If your child contracted the measles and went to school with it, the chances of transmission are incredibly high, as children don't socially distance as well as adults. A small outbreak of two or more may show up in the classroom among the children who are not vaccinated. So, your child and another now have the measles. Your little bundle of joy is making an incredibly good recovery and could be back to full health in a matter of days. The other child in the classroom is not as fortunate. The other child in the classroom now has corneal scarring and bacterial pneumonia and might not survive.

What would you think? I suppose you may think it is okay as your child is alive and not autistic. Is being autistic really something so feared that parents would rather risk their child developing severe complications that are completely preventable? It seems so.

Are cases like this rare? Absolutely! But the chance is still there. Even if it were a one in one million chance of your child developing severe complications, or transmitting a disease that could cause another to have severe complications, is that a chance you would willingly take? Another child could become seriously ill, through no fault of their own, because parents decided against vaccinations. I don't believe this is something I could live with for the rest of my life.

Was I vaccinated? Yes, I was. Thank God I haven't had any severe diseases that were entirely preventable. Am I autistic? Yes! Are the two linked? No. My parents believed that I was different even before I got vaccinated, and many other parents have stated the same. I would like to thank my wonderful parents for vaccinating me instead of putting me at risk, no matter how low, of developing lifelong disabilities.

This is a very polarizing topic that will continue to be debated for years to come.

I don't want to pretend I have all the answers. I don't. But I read and learn everything I can before I make any decisions and you should, too. The decision to vaccinate or not vaccinate is very personal but I have never, nor will I ever, encounter a death rate for autism. Nobody has died of or from autism. People do die, even today, from measles. That leaves me to draw one conclusion: people would rather risk their child's life than have them labeled autistic. What a heartbreaking conclusion it is that there are people out there who would rather have a dead child than an autistic child.

# 6

# I Found Out I Am an Autistic Adult. What Happens Now?

I have said it before and it is something that should be stressed: autism does not solely involve children! Being autistic is a lifelong honor and one simply doesn't "grow out of it." Many "naughty little children," as teachers and even their parents once called them, are diagnosed as autistic later in life. This isn't the experience that I had, as I was diagnosed at eleven years old.

I have heard many life stories from people who were diagnosed well into adulthood. The recognition of adult autism is becoming much more common and, as acceptance of the autistic mind is growing, more people are coming forward. They aren't stepping up and acknowledging that autism is part of their life because they want that "label," but to finally answer the questions of why they are different and who they truly are.

Two of the people who told me such stories were David and Jennifer. There are similarities (such as feeling that they were different from other people) and differences (beginning with the method of diagnosis) between their experiences. This is what they told me:

## David's Story

Like every autistic person, David knew that he was different. This is the classic recognition of autism, isn't it? David told me he didn't have many friends as a child and preferred to spend most of his time alone. Corporal punishment still existed in schools in the UK back in the 1970s, and he often came home from class with cane marks on his bruised, tender hands. David's teachers described him as a shy and awkward child who needed to "come out of his shell pretty quickly."

David says that making eye contact was always incredibly difficult for him. He recalled the sense of dread and fear that overcame him when his teacher would bring him up to the front of the classroom. David would leave his chair and shuffle awkwardly to the front of the classroom through a sea of deadly silence. His classmates, as well as David, knew what was coming.

David remembered being asked to discuss the themes of Shakespeare's *The Tempest* in front of his teacher and classmates. The teacher said to him, "Should you not look at and acknowledge your classmates, you shall receive five of the finest on each hand."

As David tried to look at his teacher, he became so overwhelmed that he started to cry uncontrollably. He was humiliated. The classroom was completely silent as his teacher demanded he hold out both his hands for the "finest" he was about to receive. Despite the smack of the bamboo cane across his palms, he told me that the most painful part of this ordeal was the fact that he cried in front of his entire class.

David went on to attend college and graduated as a chemical engineer. He overcame the humiliation he felt in high school and focused on his chosen career where, over the years, he successfully worked with some of the largest pharmaceutical companies in the world.

## Struggles in Adulthood

David was forty-five years old in 2008. He had worked in several places, but the jobs never lasted long. When David was telling me his story, I empathized with this somewhat. It is hard to work in a setting where your colleagues and management don't understand you. Despite a wealth of experience, knowledge, and technical skill, David was constantly disregarded and overlooked for promotion. He would have gone for interviews and given presentations to corporate CEOs, but the feedback he received was constantly negative because he wasn't "engaging enough." David knew that this was the polite way to say he didn't like having eye contact with anybody. David knew that he was the best person for the job and he knew that he had the necessary requirements to climb the corporate ladder within the company. He just couldn't "perform" the way others expected him to and he didn't really know the reason why.

David didn't know he was autistic, nor did he tell anybody what he was experiencing. How could he? He simply didn't know how to identify it. He felt he was just "odd" and was just a "shy" man who was naturally introverted.

David was also married and had two children. After a while, David's wife, Claire, raised the concern that they were having intimacy issues in their marriage, and not just issues with physical intimacy. David recalls that he became overly distant with his friends and family. He stopped meeting friends, he stopped going for happy hour after work, and he didn't discuss very much with his wife. He spent most of his time in his garage carving statuettes out of wood.

Claire worked as a schoolteacher and explained to David that he was very much like two little boys in her classroom. They didn't want to make eye contact with others but were remarkably gifted academically and very pleasant. She also told him they worked much better on their own and that she allowed them to abstain from group tasks and class presentations. She suggested that David might be autistic. At first, he admitted, he denied this possibility. He was a grown man and, to him, being autistic was only for little children.

Claire's observation planted a seed within David and he weighed and considered this possibility for several years. Like many autistic people, David didn't want to pursue a potential diagnosis. When his marriage was on the verge of collapse and his job security was feeling threatened, David knew he had to talk to someone and take positive steps for his own well-being.

## David's Action Plan

Many autistic people arrive at a fork in the road. I have discussed my own fork in the road with thousands of people and they openly share with me their similar experiences. In David's case, it was risk of marital and career collapse unless he made positive steps forward. At first, he felt reluctant to change because he thought it would be "saying goodbye to himself" or somehow emerging from the process as a different person. David viewed himself as generally successful, although he didn't know why he wasn't like his peers throughout his life. This is the outline of what David did from the moment he decided to find out "Who am I?" and not "Why am I this way?"

## Personal Research

David decided to read. David looked up several websites and books about autism and related ways of being. He read a lot of negativity and much of it resonated with him. The usual medical definitions and labels were at the forefront of internet search engines: the lack of eye contact, not being able to make friends easily, and repetitive ritualized behavior. When he read this, it hurt him deeply; he didn't want to be

viewed by everyone as being like those labels. He looked up therapies and other ways to become like the rest of society in order to not
be boxed in the autistic category. Eventually, doing his own reading
and research, he decided to visit a behavioral psychologist. At David's
insistence, for this book, he wants to highlight that this was not covered by his healthcare plan.

## Steps to Diagnosis

David finally built the courage to meet with a psychologist. He discussed his situation with the psychologist and realized that it was clear
he harbored a sense of shame as an adult for being so different as a
child. This is a common sense of embarrassment expressed by many of
us. Claire attended the psychology appointments with him to discuss
how some aspects of their marriage had been difficult. The difficulties arose not because David is autistic, but because David refused to
accept who he was and that denial caused him to withdraw from those
close to him.

Many of us do this out of fear. I certainly did! I didn't want to be
judged and placed in a derogatory category in the same way David
didn't. He believed his wife would somehow think differently of him or
shun him. This wasn't the case, as she explained that she already loved
him for who he was and that this would never change, diagnosis or not.

Eventually, David received his diagnosis in 2010 at the tender age
of forty-seven!

## Post Diagnosis

As well as being autistic, David was also seen by a psychiatrist who
diagnosed him with depression and anxiety. He began taking medication to lift his mood and feels that this has helped him greatly. David
eventually had the answer as to why nobody understood him and why

his teacher beat him, but most importantly, he had the answer of who he truly was. Deep down, he knew he was different and, after he read and researched, he had a feeling that he was autistic. In the early 1970s, autism wasn't discussed as widely as it is now. As with many who are diagnosed in adulthood, the diagnosis served to provide him with the answers to questions others had asked about him and answers to the questions he asked about himself. David views his diagnosis as a form of closure. He harbors no ill will to the colleagues or even the teachers who didn't understand him!

When David got a new job, he decided to be open about being autistic and explained to his employers that he works a certain way. Initially apprehensive about presenting himself this way, he was incredibly humbled by the accepting nature of his employer's response. When he accepted being autistic, good things happened for him.

## Jennifer's Story

It is widely recognized that autism is often underdiagnosed in the female population. In most of the groups that I visited with, the members were disproportionately men. There were some women included but not many. In one of these autistic support groups for adults, Jennifer told me her story.

Jennifer did not walk until the age of two and didn't speak until the age of four. Her earliest memory was going to a farmer's market with her father and him telling another farmer that this was his youngest, Jennifer, and she was "a bit idiot."

Jennifer grew up in a large family; her father died when she was seven years old and her mother raised her with her five brothers. They lived in poverty in a farmhouse in rural America. It was the late 1990s. Jennifer described a childhood that often left her crying in her room because she had no female company of her own age and felt quite isolated. Other than going to Sunday school and her actual school, she felt confined to her home.

Jennifer's family were devout Christians who determined her tearful tantrums were caused by her "wrong thinking" or the "sins of her parents." Jennifer's mother believed that any medical woes were the direct result of sin or transgressions of some kind. Jennifer recalled many people coming to her house to pray for her and her mother in the hope it would stop the young girl's tearful episodes.

Eventually, the tearful episodes did stop. Not because the prayer somehow worked, but because she was overwhelmed by the prayer ceremony itself. Teachers in Jennifer's school knew she did not fit in well with others even though she often tried her best to do so. When this was mentioned to her mother, the response was more prayer among the family.

As time went on, Jennifer eventually did make friends and developed a passion for art, mainly in the medium of oil painting and collage. This helped her escape from her self-perceived shortcomings and the wrath of her God-fearing family. Jennifer's family wanted her to become more involved in her church, which meant less time to focus on her passion for art. This led to many arguments at home and a strong desire and need to rebel.

Jennifer stopped going to church as frequently and defied her mother's wish to attend church activities daily after school. Jennifer was so eager to fit in that she made friends who often got her into trouble with the law. She appeared to be a confident and outgoing teen, but inside, she questioned the reason she was so different. Eventually, after some scrapes with the law, her mood began to worsen again.

Jennifer tried to tell her mother that she felt different and that she always had felt that way. Jennifer's mother ignored her plea for understanding and simply put Jennifer's feelings down as the "differing hormones" of a girl. That was not a solution to what Jennifer felt. Her questions remained, and she didn't want to defy her mother any further by going to visit a doctor without consent. She knew it was time to do some research of her own.

## A Very Different Plan

Jennifer grew up in the golden age of technology with easy access to the internet, a place where you can search for whatever you like, and Jennifer did exactly that. She knew what autism was but it wasn't until her late teens that she considered the genuine possibility that she might be autistic. The more she researched, the more convinced she became that she was autistic.

## Self-Diagnosis

I explained this in detail in an earlier chapter, but I think it is worth explaining again in the context of adults. Many charitable and voluntary groups are accepting self-diagnosed autistics. Many believe that they do not need to pay huge sums to be told what they already know.

Jennifer, like many autistic adults, does not have a formal diagnosis of autism from a medical professional. Jennifer decided to identify as autistic, as she felt she didn't require a professional to tell her what she already knew. By doing extensive research online, Jennifer found a support group near her and decided to join.

This was a group for autistic adults who met for the sole purpose of being in the company of people like them. When I visit groups, for children or adults, I always feel at home because the group members are like me. Many of the adults in Jennifer's group had gone through the same or similar experiences as she had. She could identify with them and felt no difference from the self-diagnosed members of the group and those who were traditionally diagnosed by a clinician.

When looking for information and guidance online, Jennifer opted for the information that focused on neurodiversity, as she was aware that many autism charities and causes often concentrate on the "symptoms" and negative traits that set us apart from the rest of society. Neurodiversity promotes that autism is a way of being, as opposed to a condition that needs fixing simply because we aren't like the rest.

Jennifer discussed this with her family even though they were extremely reluctant to accept her diagnosis given the strength of their faith. Jennifer, exercising her own freedom of choice, has stuck with her own diagnosis and proudly identifies as an autistic woman.

## Similarities between David and Jennifer

Everyone has their own story in terms of their autistic journey. Everyone is wonderfully unique, but many similarities remain. The common denominator is that in both cases, the individuals felt different from the rest of the world. I know and understand what that feels like because I went through the same thing. It is a feeling inside that isn't easy to describe, much like how those with epilepsy can't really describe the aura prior to a seizure.

The biggest issue among the autistic community isn't the medical model, it isn't the "symptoms" that many believe autism is, it isn't the isolation or the loneliness; it is the issue of self-acceptance. In both David's and Jennifer's experiences, refusing to accept that they were different had emotionally negative outcomes for them. It affected their mood, their self-esteem, and how they viewed their relationships with others, which impacted those relationships.

When both accepted the fact that they were autistic, they were able to make peace with themselves and move on with their lives. My experiences as an autistic person have given me a much deeper insight into other communities. I imagine this self-acceptance is like what members of the LGBT community feel when they "come out." It can be painful, but this is who you are, and acknowledging it provides a better sense of understanding yourself. Regardless of autism or anything else, you can only truly be happy when you accept yourself.

## Differences between David and Jennifer

Both David and Jennifer sought the same answer: the answer of who they are. Two perspectives came into play: the traditional route of clinical diagnosis and the self-diagnosis route. When David sought his diagnosis, he paid close to $7,500 to get the answer to the question that, deep in his heart, he already knew. Jennifer arrived at the same conclusion and it cost her nothing!

There are pluses and negatives to each perspective when we consider all ages. For children, a diagnosis is often required to receive the available help and support that is needed for school. I know this because I made use of them, even though I hated it at the time. I had a classroom assistant and extra time with teachers—which I detested, although now, in hindsight, I know that it was very much what I needed.

Whether it was because they were unable or unwilling to pay for a diagnosis, many adults I have met have been self-diagnosed. As far as additional support and resources, there isn't as much of an obligation to provide support in the workplace. In both cases, when David and Jennifer were open about themselves to their employers, the bosses were very understanding. Like any good employer should, they played to their employees' strengths to allow them to thrive.

# Conclusion

Both remarkably interesting stories and journeys traveled two very differing routes, coming to the same conclusion. They give a good insight into how diagnosis in adulthood can go. It seems that in most cases, no matter how adults are diagnosed as autistic, or self-diagnosed, they end up in the same place and are able to receive and participate in some of the same voluntary services and support groups.

I know that many readers who went on journeys like those of David and Jennifer will identify with some of the points raised within. It isn't an easy journey; it's one that I would love to make easier for absolutely everyone. I mentioned earlier that I haven't encountered any parent who has believed their child to be autistic and been wrong. I suppose this can go for adults also.

One of the many voices that have come forward to share an experience belongs to Asiatu Lawoyin. Unaware they were autistic, they followed life's path feeling disconnected from it and the people in it. This is their story, in their words.

---

## MY SUPERPOWER
### by Asiatu Lawoyin

On May 22, 2020, at the age of forty, in the midst of societal chaos and despair from a global pandemic, I was given a life-changing, self-affirming, and comforting gift. It was a present that would influence every aspect of my life. A positive among the world's negativity, and it came in the form of a social media post. I was perusing my feed as I had done many times as a means to distract myself from worry, while also keeping me informed just enough to stay educated on what was going on with the outside world. One of my online friends, who identifies as autistic, who I ironically had affectionately nicknamed "twin," had reposted a list of thirteen traits that are common among autistic girls/women. The original poster, Maxine Share, who co-manages Autism Goggles, is an autistic woman who spoke to the gender bias of autism diagnosis, resulting in girls and women being diagnosed much later in life or misdiagnosed relative to boys or men. The list of traits included

1. Weird relationship with food, may not get hungry or thirsty
2. Physically flexible
3. Can't tolerate noise
4. Love alone time
5. Socializing is draining
6. Inability to speak when emotionally overwhelmed
7. Love to write
8. Keen sense of justice
9. Feel deeply and cry easily
10. Artistic
11. Musical talent or musicality
12. Unique sense of fashion
13. Imitate behaviors of others

Every one listed applied to me. My mouth was agape and I thought to myself, "Holy sh*t! Am I autistic?" I sat there feeling seen and validated but also still in shock. I was excited and nervous. In typical autistic fashion, I then began to hyper-focus on the list and reread it a few times. I sat there and intimately thought about how each trait manifests within me. My autism journey had just begun.

The one trait that stood out the most was my food issues. I have always had a strained relationship with food. I am a picky eater, which was a source of contention with my mother in childhood. I consistently ate about twelve things and nothing else. I rarely tried new foods and most times rejected them. I have always viewed eating as a chore and felt that, if I didn't have to eat, I would do so seldom. I also rarely get hungry or thirsty. I can go all day without eating or drinking with ease, which also exacerbates my annoyance with food.

My strained relationship with my body also included painful childhood flexibility. I have always had lax joints, which were great for when I was a ballerina but awful at other times. My knees always gave me trouble because my tendons would arbitrarily become misplaced and I would lose the ability to walk. I had to get cortisone injections a few times to help aid healing, but they only worked once. Other times, I would have to sit in a warm bath attempting to straighten out my leg, which was excruciatingly painful. Also, every time my knee would become incapacitated, I would be forced to get X-rays, even though I had a history of zero breaks. In order to take the views, I would have to straighten my leg out as much as possible. It was an awful experience and happened probably approximately ten times before the age of twenty-five. At one point my mother had me medically assessed for Ehlers-Danlos syndrome, a connective tissue disorder, but I was told I didn't have enough traits.

My physical sensitivity also included my noise intolerance. The loud sounds of school, including the bell to change classes, the screeching of the chairs on the floor, as well as the students' voices, especially at recess and dismissal, always made me feel inner turmoil. I felt overstimulated and I wanted to go somewhere quiet to have some peace, but being so young I couldn't quite express or understand my angst. When older, going into large festivals, people's chatter evoked that cringey feeling like many experience when hearing nails on a chalkboard. Sound volume isn't the only aspect of my noise sensitivity; I also despise repetitive sound. I hated listening to the second hand of the clock ticking in class. To me, at times, it was deafening and I struggled to stay focused on the teacher.

The noise of school wasn't the only part that overwhelmed me. Socializing was also draining. My absolute favorite thing has always been sleeping. As a kid, I would fall asleep so often on anything moving, to self-regulate, that my mother would tease me affectionately as having "car-colepsy." There were many field trip bus rides in kindergarten that the teachers were unable to wake me up and I would have to be carried back into the school. Looking back, it was the utter noise and chaos of the bus, especially on the return trip or after socializing, that would trigger a shutdown for me.

Other times, I would dissociate when overburdened by emotion, such as when in a disagreement. I would become involuntarily mute. Another example is public speaking; I have always hated it. One memory of being speechless is when I was in sixth grade. It was a private school that I only attended for its last year because my public school transferred the sixth grade to middle school the year after I graduated fifth grade. The majority of the students had known each other for many years. It only heightened my sense of feeling like an outsider and all I wanted to do was to blend in. However, this particular day, my English teacher began class by anonymously commending a student's essay that was "comparable to a high school student." She continued for a few minutes praising this student's writing ability. She said she was going to ask the person to come read it in front of the class. I was comforted that it couldn't be me so I had nothing to worry about. I didn't think my writing was that exemplary.

However, then she spoke my name and I wanted the floor to open and swallow me. I was in absolute shock. My heart began palpitating and I didn't think I would be able to speak at all, let alone in front of my classmates. However, I pushed through my anxiety, focused only on the paper in my trembling hands, and begrudgingly read my essay while wanting to die in that moment. Though I despised being put on the spot, that teacher solidified my love of writing, which continued and flourished in college at Spelman where I graduated with a bachelor's of sociology, which included my thesis. Even today, as a professional empowerment coach, all of my sessions are online via chat or text.

Though I have always enjoyed writing, including adolescent creative stories, I struggled with the logistics before computers became the norm. I found the physicality of writing difficult, and in high school I was medically diagnosed with "significant weakness in my visual motor integration," or dyspraxia.

My otherness, combined with my keen sense of justice, has always connected me to the oppressed. I also have always felt things deeply, which is at the root of my ability to empathize with others. I have always cried at Disney movies, no matter how many times I've seen them. I remember the first time I went to the movies to see *E.T.* and at the end I stood up on my seat, tears streaming down my face, shouting, "Don't go E.T., don't go!"

My emotional sensitivity is also at the center of my life-coaching business. Being a black person, and raised in a social activist family, combined with my sense of feeling like an alien, I have always wanted to help others find healing and justice. I also have always been hyperaware of others' suffering and can identify with people that feel like their voice isn't heard, understood, or validated. I work with marginalized groups, specializing in the neurodiverse, as a means to combat that reality. I also am an ally educator to assist evolution from both sides.

My artistic and creative nature isn't limited to my business, but it also permeates all aspects of who I am, including my unique and personal style of fashion, writing, and musicality. I have always used clothes as a means to express my independence. I remember in seventh grade I decided that I wanted to wear ties to my all-girls, predominately white middle school on free dress days. I also love creating as a means for people to have a better understanding of each other and foster connection. From writing creative stories in elementary school, to falling in love with high school art class, to teaching preschool kids using the Creative curriculum, I have always incorporated art. I also have a strong connection to music as it helps soothe my soul in times of despair. I also remember things via song, such as childhood jingles that randomly come to mind, even as an adult.

Though my artistic expression is unique and I am quite independent in nature, as a child especially, I struggled with my social understanding. I always looked to my peers for social cues such as the standards of fashion that I would then imitate before accenting in my own way or expressing in my own style. Also, I would look to others as guides of socializing because I have always hated social norms and niceties, as well as having struggled with expressing myself in blunt ways that are deemed socially inappropriate.

After allowing my brain to process the list and then further affirm my beliefs through much more research, while validating so many of my past experiences, I was comfortable claiming a self-diagnosis of autism. I then decided to pursue a medical diagnosis and, after some initial difficulties finding a therapist that I felt was knowledgeable and suited me, on Oct 2, 2020, at age forty-one, my belief was affirmed. I received a medical diagnosis of autism. My entire life I have felt like an alien and now I have the reason why. I am autistic and it is my superpower!

---

I have met numerous young adults in their early twenties and thirties. They knew, or learned, what autism was and were able to identify with it. When I asked if they, deep down inside themselves, believed they were autistic, they all confirmed emphatically that they did. As a clinically diagnosed autistic, I don't see them as any less than me. Nobody should. Their discovery and the recognition of it brought about an appreciation of their individual differences.

One of those adults, who began by learning about autism and developed until it eventually led to a diagnosis, hit very close to home for me. Adrian Newcastle was the narrator of my first book and, through a series of synchronicities, including coming into contact with me, made a series of discoveries that validated what he had long felt. Those discoveries allowed him to identify with his true self and redefine his life. The following is Adrian's story of discovery, which he has graciously provided to illustrate how one can go through the early stages of life without a diagnosis.

---

## DISCOVERY AND WHAT LED TO IT
### by **Adrian Newcastle**

### August 2020

It is said that the closer you come to a black hole, the faster you need to go to maintain escape velocity and so avoid gravity's pull across the threshold of the event horizon. In terms of my formal autism diagnosis, I feel as if I have been circling that event horizon for the last thirty years. Eventually, I ran out of forward momentum and the gravity of the situation became inescapable. I crossed the threshold.

### May 14, 1983

I was eight years old and critically injured in a bike accident after school. I was rushed to the hospital for emergency surgery to repair a perforated bowel and massive internal bleeding. Though I was not expected to survive the night, I pulled through. I was heavily sedated with morphine for the first four days of my two-week stay, which may relate to later problems. This was the first of two major surgeries for me. As I lived a rural life, I was an active child, though I was not the same afterwards. I began to develop chronic back pain issues in my teens. Still, I was hypermobile and had excellent balance and hand-eye coordination, which were advantages for the trade I went into as a painting contractor.

## July 1997

I had been married nearly a year at this point, and while my wife knew I was quirky, it did not take long to discern that some of my nontypical social behaviors were not things I could unlearn. To her vast credit she did not try to force me into a mold of her own making. At this time the internet provided a new resource and, for the first time, I was able to do a little digging into what exactly was wrong with me. It was no secret that I was not like other people. I knew it; they knew it. I worked hard to provide what I thought was appropriate social feedback, but the gap was wide.

I'm not the first one to write this particular thought, but my research (which mainly involved questionnaires and social tests) indicated that I was apparently a psychopath!

That was genuinely bizarre as I had no harmful tendencies and was, in fact, very interested and active in volunteer work to help people. So just what was going on?

I knew by now that nine-to-five employment did not work. As a solution I subcontracted my trade skills and found regular part-time work in another city. One client was a nice married couple with two children. While I was working at their house the oldest child came home from school and was visibly unsettled by strangers working in the home.

The mother was not flustered in any way, but explained to us that he (the child) was autistic, had been diagnosed with Asperger's, and found the work in the home a little overwhelming. As she described more about the condition, I made a mental note to look it up.

I did not do much research on the topic; after I saw that I fell into all the Asperger's boxes instead of the psychopath ones, that was good enough for me. Whether or not I was autistic did not matter; my curiosity was satisfied.

## October 10, 2004

It has been twenty-one years since my bike accident, and the cumulative effects from that and my hypermobility were manifesting themselves in negative ways in the course of my work. I found I needed regular physical therapy in order to continue. On my way to a treatment I was injured in a hit-and-run car accident. I was not at fault, yet the consequences have been permanent.

## September 2018

My injuries from that accident, though not severe, were bad enough. Life became progressively more difficult and I was diagnosed with fibromyalgia in 2012, requiring a change of job. I switched trades to a lighter-duty activity and operated a commercial window-cleaning route.

Since my youth, I had always maintained part-time self-employment. By now I had come to see that the reason I was self-employed did not lie solely with my injuries. The problem was people, new environments, sheer exhaustion, and sometimes simply not wanting to get out of the car. Even the marketing and social interaction of this new trade became crippling at times. I started to have panic issues when my phone rang.

Without those two accidents and subsequent health issues, I would not have started to seriously look at using some of my skills to pursue narration work. The reality was that I was losing forward momentum to keep escaping what it seemed I did not want to be my reality. Now, in my forties, the physical and mental stress was aggravating the fibromyalgia, which, in turn, made masking just about impossible. I thought voice-over or narration could be a job I could do. I figured it would take three years to be able to get it off the ground while I continued window cleaning.

## May 2019

What was supposed to be a three-year plan instead became an instant plan due to market conditions. I needed to leave the cleaning behind me and go all in on the narration. My contractual obligations in cleaning tied me up until May 26, 2019.

This date may not have significance to any readers but one: Jude Morrow. The date of our contract to do the audio for his first book is May 27, 2019.

Jude, a newly minted self-published author, crossed paths with Adrian, a newly minted audiobook narrator. Both had lived a life with autism. Only one of them was diagnosed. Were it not for my physical challenges, I would not have been looking into narration at all. Had I not been looking for narration work, I would not have auditioned for the most oddly titled book I had seen on the audition platform, in an Irish accent no less! Had I not auditioned, I would not have had a reckoning with my autism.

From the audition script I had no clue as to what the book was about or that Jude had autism. I didn't learn that until I was sent the full manuscript to read. I had made no mention to Jude about my own possible connection.

The audition script was snippets from three different chapters with no context. What had at first been a simple throw-away audition to test my Irish speaking skills had now become a puzzle. These did not appear to be completely random selections, and the book was clearly speaking from the author's personal experience. What did they mean?

While I have had no formal acting training, I—like many autistic people—have had a lifetime of experience in masking. I used this to mimic which emotion I thought may fit each scene. I have no idea how many submissions Jude received or why he chose me, though I'm pretty sure it was not because I had the most outstanding Irish accent!

As each (audio) chapter was complete I sent it to Jude for review.

I realized something very quickly. While Jude's childhood experience with autism was very different from mine, and his external traits were dissimilar to mine, at the core, I resonated very deeply with what he wrote. It was as if he was writing me. I found this concerning.

I had expected accent issues to correct, and there were a few. What disturbed me is that as chapters were turned in, Jude kept telling me that I captured the emotion exactly. I expressed it as he felt it. How could that be, as Jude was autistic? I clearly seemed to "get" what he was writing. Why was that?

I was being confronted with my own autism in a very unexpected and unplanned way.

I did my best at the time. I do not know if those who are not on the spectrum feel that I have all the emotional cues and intonations all wrong. What I found as I progressed through the work is that the wider audience did not matter to me. Since this was a very personal story, I decided that I only needed to make one person happy, and that was Jude.

How does one read and emote emptiness and hollowness inside? How do you express in voice the pain of a life on the outside looking in? As it turns out, I was able to put myself in his shoes, not through shared expressions of the autistic condition or activities, but through shared battles.

I started to work on building a network in an online business-to-business platform by which to introduce people to Jude's work, as I thought he had an important message to share. Through this process I became acquainted with a whole community of people who are like me, and I am like them. It's as if I have been speaking life as a second language for thirty years and I have now found my homeland and my people. This interaction started to change my thinking.

## November 2019

I was still circling, yet, as I got closer to it, I started to discern that there was possibly something good across the threshold of the event horizon. I began to consider that I may be able to contribute more to the support of others on the spectrum if I did get a formal diagnosis.

From time to time it is good to reflect that it is not all about us. Our autism may be having a profound effect on our family and friends in ways that we simply do not understand or even notice. Even when it is explained, we may still not comprehend it. We do not have to understand something to accommodate it. We simply have to understand that the expressions made to us about its effects are genuine, and if there is something we can do to help, we should.

I brought the matter up to my doctor again, a little more seriously, to suss out the process to a formal diagnosis. I did not go farther, as I had other more pressing health concerns to deal with at the time. It simmered on the back burner until life came to a screeching halt.

## March 2020

COVID-19 brought with it a digital conferencing tool, which became ubiquitous. I just can't do it. It produces a very unpleasant physical reaction. I have never liked or used video chat of any sort, but this was a whole different animal.

Being a practical sort of person, my solution was simply to use audio only. Apparently, people want to see me. I do not understand this particularly well (I can hear them and process their information just fine without video) but the fact remains they wondered where I had vanished.

There comes a time in life when you just get tired of explaining things. I may have reached this a few decades early.

I think many autistic people understand what I mean when I state that masking is exhausting. When I was younger, I had energy to deal with this. After the fibromyalgia set in, this became progressively more difficult. If I do not have the energy to mask, then my ability to speak graciously diminishes. In person I would just exit the situation and find a space to recharge and hope that I have not offended anyone in the meantime.

I realized quickly that we were in for a long haul, and to be able to move forward in this new conferencing environment, it would be the least hassle and best if I just formalized my diagnosis, whatever that may turn out to be, autism or otherwise. My forward inertia to escape the diagnosis was finally spent and gravity did what gravity does, and so across the threshold I went.

## October 2020

I have to say it was a weight lifted. Mainly because it brought home something I simply was not seeing: the effect that my autism had on my wife. I did not see the burden she was carrying all these years, trying to smooth out my interactions with others. She has never resented me for this and for that I am truly grateful. She is relieved now that she can explain that how I communicate is different. As I worked my way through Jude's account, I started to think that his parents and sister deserved a gold star for the challenges they faced when he was young.

I feel the same way about my wife and others who provide stability to family members on the spectrum. Without their support, love, and patience the opportunity for autistic voices and ideas to be heard would be greatly diminished. It must never be taken for granted.

My own family has been accepting of the news. For most of them it was like all of my quirky behaviors fell into place.

As the occasion arises, my wife has been letting our friends know and the most common answer has literally been exactly the same in each case.

"You mean you didn't know?"

Much like Jude, who thought he was masking so well until he finally revealed his Asperger's at work, I, too, was no mystery to those around me who had been exposed to autism through their own family or work circumstances.

Overall, I firmly believe much better times are ahead. The digital age has allowed communication between autistics on a scale that simply did not exist thirty years ago. When knowledge is shared, understanding is gained. When understanding is gained, communication can begin. When communication begins, ideas are exchanged. When ideas are exchanged, anything is possible.

---

If you are reading this book and identify with many of the points raised and think, "This is me," then you are probably right. It is nothing to be afraid of. Like us, you can love your place on the spectrum, too. If it is the case that you are part of our community, I am only too happy to formally welcome you to the club!

# 7

## Do I *Have* Autism or Am I *Autistic*?

Since becoming an advocate for all things regarding autism and neurodiversity, I have had the pleasure of speaking to more people like me. We always have common ground, and if there is a shared special interest with someone I am talking to, video chats and interviews can stretch far beyond allocated time slots, sometimes by hours! Not all the conversations revolve around our special topics and mutual interests; many go much deeper than that. In the discussions I was having, I learned to listen to others because I realized that we all must start our journey somewhere and that very few of us have identical views. I shared my thoughts on what being an advocate meant to me, and my conversation friends told me what they thought an advocate should be. We basically agreed that autistic advocacy should be about highlighting what generally undermines or limits the autistic community, but doing so in a kind and gentle manner that allows people to see the other side—our side—of the topic. Any advocate who behaves in a way that deters people from seeking advice or support should not presume the title of advocate at all. That perception was fairly unanimous.

Imagine how surprised I was when some told me that I was part of the problem without even realizing that I was at fault. It was all because of verbiage I hadn't realized is offensive and hurtful to some.

Many parents have asked me what terminology they should use when they discuss their child. They want to know, "Is my child *autistic* or do they *have* autism?" It's a fierce debate, and there seem to be two very different thoughts on the matter. The majority of the autistic community champions use of the term "autistic" to demonstrate pride in their identity. However, there are those who prefer to say they have autism, even though many autistic people find that language hurtful. Generally, those who are not autistic use the terminology "having autism." They might use the words in a description such as, "That man on the stage is Jude Morrow. And he has autism."

In the book *Why Does Daddy Always Look So Sad?* I state that I have autism. I did that as a means of explaining my differences, which, as most neurodiverse and neurotypical people experience, can present a negative perspective. Eventually I shifted my thinking. Instead of viewing my life as a constant struggle or believing that I was a burden to those trying to help me, I realized—and, for the first time, appreciated—the fact that I am resilient and capable of achieving many good things. I had to retrain my thinking to understand that the remarkable things in the present moment of my life completely overshadowed what I viewed as a devastating hurricane of negativity surrounding my childhood and early adulthood.

Also, the language used in *Why Does Daddy Always Look So Sad?* is the language that I was brought up with and that I had heard all the time. I used the language that was mainstream without realizing the negative connotations it had for some of my readers, mainly those who had knowledge of neurodiversity. I didn't know what neurodiversity was at that time, and I had no idea that certain uses of words and language were offensive to my fellow autistics.

What I have since learned is that people "having autism" seems to be the default language of the entire world! Everywhere I look and read there are descriptions of children and adults *with* autism. For many years, I overlooked this and thought that if it is published online in books, journals, and research papers, surely it must be the accepted language and terminology.

As time went by, and I had the opportunity to speak to young and old autistic people, I learned more and more about the autistic community and their preferences. Connecting with them is always a wonderful experience because there's an undercurrent of unspoken understanding between each other that I don't have the words to describe. The best I can do is to equate it to telepathy or a sixth sense of some type. We tend to openly discuss things between us because we know there is no judgment. One of the best things I learned from my many discussions was that the language I was using was part of the problem! When I wrote blog posts and had media interviews following the debut of my book, I used the language the medical model employs. Autistic people find that offensive because most of us don't feel *afflicted with* something to be treated or cured. It's just a way of life for us and we own it.

When one advocate challenged my choice of language, she informed me that terms like this were hurtful to her and also to other autistic people. I was shocked! What was wrong with using the verbiage I had always known and used? I wasn't certain how to react, but when I feel I am being criticized, I tend to get a little defensive and retaliate with a question back to them. I inquired why people would find my words offensive. I am not one to invalidate someone's opinion or feelings on the spot; instead, I'm prompted to listen to what they say and then research their points much more thoroughly.

The same advocate explained to me that those individuals and groups in the medical model had used the outdated nomenclature and symbolism for autistics. That is the model that focuses on cures and changes for autistic people. At that point I didn't know that there was anything but the medical model, so I set about further research. I learned about neurodiversity; I learned about choices the autistic community prefers as opposed to those made by the neurotypical. I also learned that advocacy and education create a ripple effect like a stone dropped in a pond. Someone made me aware of these issues and now I pass it on to you, with a hope that you will do the same for someone else.

As an avid reader and writer, I understand the impact that words can have on people. Even the most basic words can have a profound influence on those who read them or hear them. It's not always about context; sometimes it's just about perception and the way the word makes you feel. Words, and the implications they leave us with, can easily create insult or upset. Shifting the conceptualization of a word or phrase alters the underlying sentiment toward it. This couldn't be any truer than within the autistic community when it comes to the "I am autistic" versus "I have autism" debate.

I am the first to admit that I didn't always refer to myself as an autistic person. I would have said that I have autism. But I have learned from the autistic community that they prefer to say that they are autistic. After I listened to these autistic voices, researched, and understood why it was their preference, I made the same choice and empathize with why that term is preferred. The reason is simple: we are proud of our identity. I am proud to be autistic and believe everyone should be proud of who they are. Feeling deficient in what society expects of us has not served us well. I look back on what I now consider wasted years because I felt ashamed of all the things that somebody else thought were wrong with me. I believed that I needed help and support to normalize and survive instead of celebrating my own identity and differences. After all, I had been told that over and over.

As a practicing social worker, I am a professional with many years' experience. I have referred to someone as a "person with dementia," a "person with osteoarthritis," or a "person with Parkinson's disease." Those references are all to people who acquired an illness or disease due to many medical justifications, including age. I have even used this terminology when describing a service user I work with. Parents and professionals say things like "with autism" and "with ASD" to demonstrate that the person being spoken about *is a person first*, and the label doesn't define who they are as a person. I don't understand this sentiment. We prefer *identity first* language. We are autistic people, in the same way one wouldn't say "a person with gay" or "a person with French."

Rather than limit my knowledge to one model, I chose to visit with numerous autism groups and trained professionals because I needed to gain their perspectives, too. I needed to understand the difference between "having autism" and "being autistic." What I learned opened my eyes, mind, and heart to who we, the autistic community, really are. What is the difference? All the above-mentioned diagnoses are profoundly serious medical conditions that have been acquired in the middle to latter stages of life. Being autistic isn't like that. It is an intrinsic part of our being from birth. Yes, people can be born with serious medical conditions that require ongoing medical and nursing treatment, and that includes many autistic people, too. The difference is that being autistic means that we are simply another diversity group that generally doesn't need to be recognized or treated in a drastically different manner than others. We are not diseased, disordered, or dreadful. We are just different. Yes, we will probably need some help and direction, but we don't need to be coddled or cured. We need to be appreciated for who we are, which might include behavior that some might find disconcerting. If you look past the little things that may seem odd, we are just like everyone else. We are human, with emotions and wide-ranging feelings that we may not show like everyone else, but they are there and they are real to us. I am autistic, and I promise it doesn't have to be a sentence of doom and gloom! We have good days and bad days just like every other human. It seems strange that we live in a society that embraces unique quirkiness and yet tries its best to fix us even though we aren't broken.

This topic wasn't well explored or even debated until recently, but it is starting to be a subject of important discussions. This is a debate which is very much welcome in my view. A room full of people who have a personal or professional connection with autism will never agree totally on what terminology is best to use. Have I met autistic people who prefer to say they "have" autism? In fact, there are those who prefer that. But there are also individuals, advocacy groups, and platforms fueled by autistic voices saying that the term "having" autism is offensive.

As more and more autistic people provide their perspectives on verbal definitions, things will change, in much the same way Martin Luther King Jr. advocated for civil rights. I, like many advocates for autism, am a proponent for a type of right. It might not equate to Martin Luther King Jr.'s struggles, but for our community it is just as real. I am fortunate to have experienced both sides of the equation and heard both sides of the discussion. I understand the pain that is caused by professionals, particularly from the medical community, who say that using the terms "ASD" or "having Autism" is not offensive. They should allow us to speak for ourselves. That is where neurodiversity is helpful. It is designed to let us be comfortable in our own skin, which means that the discussion and debate should expand among all people. Eventually, a term will be settled on and it will take hold and propagate until it becomes universally recognized. Until then, I am proud to say, "I am autistic!"

All one needs to do is research surveys among the autistic community to find out which terminology is preferred. In many (if not all) studies, the winner is "autistic person." I have yet to encounter a global movement of autistic people that advocates for the "having autism" verbiage. Many autistic-led groups are proud and vocal in their belief that they don't need to be fixed. I take my proverbial hat off to them. It is very disheartening when someone tells you the language that offends you isn't offensive at all. Am I not allowed to decide? I am not a wallflower or delicate soul, but when a large section of the autistic community is saying that terminology is offensive, this cannot and should not be ignored.

Some parents take the approach that their children do prefer saying that they "have autism." In a way, each person has their own individual preference and that is fine and should be considered. The difficult thing with children, especially autistic children, is self-advocacy. As a child, if someone told me to put my hand into a fire to fit in and be like everyone else, I would have done it without question. As a child, I was certainly compliant and constantly sought approval from everyone else. If professionals labeled me as "a vile human being," I would have gone along with it because that's what I would have believed everyone expected of me. Sometimes I still hide behind the feelings of my childlike self. When I was small, I loved playing with my toy cars. I carried them everywhere with me and lined them up. I find myself lining up Ethan's toy cars and using the excuse that I am simply tidying them up for him, instead of embracing my innocent little urge to have them in an orderly fashion. Some things never change. But if you are an autistic child and someone tags you with a label that you find uncomfortable, speak up. Do not allow anyone to use language that makes you feel uncomfortable. The rest of us in the community will have your back . . . always!

There is a point that needs to be made for each of us in the autistic community. We are individuals but we are not victims unless we choose to be victims. Terminology can make one feel like a victim, especially when it is words being used to define you that you don't identify with. Don't accept what you don't feel. Stand up and state which words you use to describe yourself. As they say today, own it. Be proud of it, and don't let anyone make you feel less than you are.

My view of "with autism" is that it almost seems like a term someone came up with to be polite. When people describe people "with autism," it is like they can be separated from autism somehow. That is impossible. I firmly believe that education and a broader spectrum of available information will alter the accepted usage from "having autism" to "being autistic," the term that appears to be more acceptable to the community.

When I am speaking or acting as an advocate for others, people see and feel the excitement of the moment—or the response that gets a round of applause, for example. The most difficult thing about advocacy is what an advocate hears. I have to hear it all—and not just *hear* it; I have to listen carefully to what is being said and the emotion behind it. I hear wonderful, positive, and uplifting stories, and sadly, I hear the odd comments that find their way in, too. I shook my head in disbelief when someone said to me that saying "autistic" is the same as saying someone is "cancerous" instead of "having cancer." That statement was so astronomically ridiculous that I can't even begin to wrap words around it. It all boils down to pathologizing autistic people. Autism is simply a difference, not a progressive disease that would be fatal if left untreated.

People have different senses; most are aware of the six senses, while neurologists say we have between nine and twenty including acceleration, direction, and pain. As I have said, autistic people perceive and interact with the world differently; we perceive and relate to sensory structure differently than most people. That does not mean we are ill or that we can be altered to relate to the world in a different way.

Welcome ASD (autism spectrum disorder) to the stage. People say someone "is" ASD or "has" ASD. It's the same debate as I just presented: "I am" or "I have." The word "disorder" is the most troubling word in this definition; autism is a disorder to whom? The answer is also the same that I have repeated throughout the pages of this book. It's a disorder to the neurotypical majority. As a proud and defiant collective, autistic people only have a "disorder" according to the neurotypical masses. Take a moment; pause and think about how abstract the term "disorder" sounds to us. The word means a lack of organization, or contributing to the breakdown of law-abiding behavior. We might appear disorganized to some but we, like every other human, do things in our own way and, quite often, with great success.

Here is an analogy. If there is one thing in life I love, it is fiery English mustard. I never go without it; I lather it onto my bacon or sausage sandwiches, and I'm also partial to corned beef! If there are one hundred people in a room and eighteen of the people hate mustard and the rest love it, which group has a disorder?

Would the group with the disorder be the eighty-two people who love spicy mustard? Probably not. They would be the neurotypical people who could get away with saying that the condiment might be too potent for the delicate taste buds of the eighteen. Do the eighteen people who dislike mustard have a disorder? Would it be called Hating Mustard Disorder (HMD)? The majority, consisting of the eighty-two people who love mustard, could easily make a blanket declaration that those eighteen have something wrong with them. Carrying my little daydream analogy further, I could imagine that if there were an HMD diagnosis added to medical textbooks and diagnostic manuals, there would be a slew of Board-Certified Mustard Therapists who cropped up overnight to solve the disorder and claim a therapy or cure for HMD. The therapy might consist of a treatment that gives a reward every time you have a spoonful of mustard. It would require therapy for forty hours a week and would absolutely cure everyone of their distaste for fiery mustard. The Board-Certified Mustard Therapists would have created a diagnostic criterion for something that is literally unknown to them because they love fiery mustard.

Now examine the people who have been grouped and labeled with HMD. Like most groupings that have a pathology attached to them, those "with HMD" will eventually question the nomenclature of the term. They may advocate and campaign that their dislike for fiery mustard is simply their choice and should be respected. Eventually, there may be a Mustard Advocacy Network established worldwide that defies the majority decision to make people like mustard equally. If there were such a thing, I would support it, even though I love mustard. Those who don't like mustard don't need to be repaired. They need to be understood and accepted as they are.

I know that my imaginative HMD thoughts may sound like a ridiculous concept, but it is comparable to what has happened with autistic people around the world. In this case, we are the people who don't like mustard in our sandwiches while the majority does like it. Though I cannot fathom why anyone would omit the fiery bliss of mustard from their meat, I would never think that those who do leave mustard on the shelf are somehow deficient or require training to eat mustard. This all goes back to the word "disorder." People with differing sensory levels interact with the world differently.

The issue of verbiage is also true when people say they know someone who "suffers" from autism. I do not, nor have I ever, suffered from autism. I suffered from low self-esteem, depression, anxiety, and compliant behaviors *because I felt deficient*. All I ever tried to do was communicate in the ways I recognized and understood, even though they weren't good enough to some others. That is not reason enough for anyone to suffer emotionally; at least, that is my opinion.

Being autistic is a huge part of my identity. It always was but I just didn't realize it until later in my life. It is who I am. Some people say that being autistic doesn't define them. That's okay, too. People don't have to identify with or conform to anything that they don't want to. That is perfectly acceptable to me, but being autistic is central to my notion of identity and I don't want this taken away from me.

When discussing this topic with others, I often hear that everyone is entitled to their own opinion, followed by an offer to agree to disagree. I generally don't do that. I can be opinionated, but always my opinion is based on and around support for the autistic community and the individuals that comprise it. The few times I resort to agreeing to disagree are when the other half of the debate is completely unreasonable. Trying to reason with someone who is unreasonable is exhausting. Since the majority of the autistic community prefers to use the term "autistic," I support that and utilize that terminology. It is seen as much more progressive, and all the stigmas have been detached from it.

Shouldn't we, through discussion as a community, decide what language hurts us? Shouldn't this discussion and decision be community led? Many autistic people would love to see the textbooks and teaching support tools changed to reflect the language that is most acceptable and less hurtful to us. Why do so many professionals ignore the clients they are supposed to serve by denying the client's right to highlight language and terminology that is hurtful to them? There aren't many groups and services designed by autistic people—at least, not many that are in the mainstream on a global level. That means that neurotypical thinking has produced the concepts of what we need. It is all completely baffling to me.

The journey of autism advocacy has allowed me to empathize with and understand the frustrations of all human and civil rights campaigners who ever lived. I know of numerous neurodiversity advocates who actively campaign to remove language that many of us find hurtful. (It's even more hurtful when we are told that it "isn't offensive.") Judgment doesn't eliminate a problem. It only cloaks it in ignorance. The mission each and every one of us should aspire to is to be accepted and accept others, too. Imagine a group of people stating that certain descriptive terms were not accurately portraying them. Most people would become more sensitive to the group's feelings and their response to the terminology. It's just being considerate of fellow humans. We should be doing that for each other anyway.

Here are the primary points for autistic and non-autistic people to recognize:

∞ A large portion of the autistic community finds the term "having autism" offensive and negative.

∞ The "autistic versus having autism" discussion should not be a debate. It is more accurate to state that one is autistic, but we should accept the choice of the autistic individual.

∞ Autistic voices matter! Listen to them, please.

∞ Many people and professionals have good intentions but use the kind of language that they were taught . . . the negative kind.

∞ It is never too late to shift perspectives.

∞ I love spicy mustard.

# 8

# Generally Accepted Therapies

Around the world, many clinicians and practitioners offer treatments for autistic children and adults. Have I undergone various therapies as an autistic person? Yes, I have, and I found them very beneficial. For me, therapy didn't involve changing who I was or my way of being, but rather it helped me accept and love myself.

Therapies and treatments have existed for autistic people since the beginning of psychiatric and psychological care; most have become widespread since the end of World War II and the beginning of the 1950s. Individuals, like me, who have undergone therapies to accept themselves generally flourish. Those who went through the more antiquated therapies designed to change a specific pattern or way of being have experienced mixed results.

Opinions on various therapies are so wide-ranging that they could have a spectrum all their own—one that is actually much larger than the autistic community. I have met men and women and children who praise certain therapies, and then there are those who vehemently oppose them. I am glad to hear that autistic voices are getting louder

and expressing their thoughts on therapies. I hope those voices will continue to grow louder, but each individual considering therapy should
examine all aspects of it and hear from autistic people who support and
oppose a specific therapy.

I am not providing a peer-reviewed analysis of each and every therapy that exists in the world. I speak of my experience, share the stories
that I've been told, and present others who openly share their experiences. Some have had positive experiences; others, not so much. That
said, the actual focus of this chapter is not just therapy but how everyone, autistic or not, can move forward toward acceptance.

## Stimming

Self-stimulatory behavior, known colloquially as stimming, is the repetition of self-regulatory movements, sounds, and movements of objects.
Stimming is not just limited to the autistic community, but it is prevalent
there. Twisting one's hair, unconsciously wiggling one's foot, or tapping
one's fingers are all forms of self-stimulatory behavior that are common.
The general public considers those non-disruptive. Stimming serves to
soothe and comfort. It can also be used to block excess sensory input or
to provide extra sensory input when needed. In its own way, especially
for our community, it is a type of therapy. When I was a child, I often
repeated words under my breath and loved lining up my toy cars on
my windowsill. Even now, I find organizing things quite therapeutic,
but only in particular circumstances. I will be the first to admit that I am
not always incredibly organized regarding my own house. (Yes, autistic
people can have mess and clutter, just like everyone else.)

Repetition and self-regulation stimming are not to be confused
with obsessive-compulsive disorder (OCD), wherein actions are often
completed out of fear as opposed to happening naturally and without

thinking. Quite often my son tells me that I repeated what I just said under my breath even though I didn't even realize it.

As I said in the first chapter, I can often be found pacing up and down the stage prior to a show. I correlate the words I have to say with how many steps I can take across the stage and back again. I suppose this could be counted as stimming, as well. I was never one to flap my arms and hands at school, although this type of stimming is a very common autistic feature. Stimming on the whole is viewed as harmless and perfectly okay within the autistic community, although teachers and other pupils find it distracting.

There can be other stims that are harmful, and intervention is required to reduce the risk of injury or worse. Head banging and scratching oneself or others can be very challenging for all involved. Stimming can be reactionary and happen in moments of excitement and in moments of anger or frustration. In cases like this, it is important to identify the triggers that lead to the detrimental action and create safer stimming habits.

## Applied Behavior Analysis—ABA

ABA is a variant of behavioral engineering. It's often recommended to parents as a means to curb stimming and other activities so that a child isn't disruptive to the rest of society. O. Ivar Lovaas used electric shocks to stop children from engaging in their obsessive, repetitive behaviors.[4] He felt equal amounts of reward and punishment could sculpt a better-behaved child. Since then ABA has frequently been used as a type of intervention for autistic children in mainstream schools, as well as special education schools. As the name suggests, the primary goal of behavioral engineering is to modify and improve behaviors that are deemed "not normal" or not socially acceptable.

This type of behavior modification can be traced back to the 1950s, when it was promoted as a rewards-based system. If one complied with what was considered normal, one was rewarded. ABA wasn't specifically formulated for autism; it has been used in other circumstances like eating disorders and as a conversion therapy for those in the LGBT community.

The generally accepted process is focused on a child who has demonstrated what may be viewed as difficult behavior. That may include things such as hand flapping, repeating words under their breath, or pacing around a room. Under ABA, these require some form of intervention to stop the activity. From the stories I have heard, the normal regimen of ABA requires approximately forty hours per week, give or take a few hours. This can be done at home or within the classroom environment, where the reward and punishment systems are implemented to reduce or eradicate behaviors that are very difficult to alter or stop.

ABA is said to have a market size of approximately $17 billion in the United States alone. That is a huge number. With the creation of newer ABA accreditations, programs, and "therapies," this number is likely to grow much larger. What is also concerning is the rise of online learning and development. I did a little bit of research into how one can become an ABA therapist, and the results were absolutely staggering. In one program, there was no university degree required, and no experience or certifications in child development were necessary. All that was needed was a basic secondary education and some money, and not a lot of that. I found courses ranging from costing absolutely nothing to some with fees that were quite substantial amounts. Some autism support groups even offer to train ABA therapists for a small fee. There are university-accredited programs, but some do not require a degree of any kind and are certifications that are basically purchased online. How does that help anyone?

It is the little children, the pride and joy of parents, who are most often the subjects of ABA "treatment." No matter what type of therapy is being considered, I urge parents to verify the credentials before you entrust your child to an "expert." Don't trust website endorsements as a sole reason for signing up for something. Anyone can create a website that makes them appear knowledgeable. Do some research; speak to people who have participated and find out what their experiences were. Website endorsements may or may not be valid. It's up to us to check claims that sound too good to be true, because very often they are just that . . . too good to be true.

The bottom line is this: a therapy that indicates that your wonderful child *needs* to be a certain way to be accepted by their peers should be avoided at all costs.

## ABA Today

If families, individuals, and groups heard some of the stories I have heard, they might view ABA more like torture than a therapy. Today more and more therapists and clinicians with a working knowledge of ABA argue against using it. Articles in magazines and online explain the reasons it is being examined more closely. Spectrum ran an article headlined "The Controversy over Autism's Most Common Therapy."[5] According to a study published in *Advances in Autism*, nearly half of children and adults exposed to ABA experienced post-traumatic stress disorder (PTSD).[6]

Fortunately, our community is speaking up and telling their stories so that those outside our community realize what type of trauma we experience when we undergo some of the more conventional therapies. The scars may not show immediately, but for many they are carried through life. JayJay Mudridge is one of those who stepped forward to share the lasting effects of ABA (facebook.com/notanotherautisticadvocate/). They share their traumatic story below and calls it "Reverberations." (This story may be difficult to read, but experiences like this need to be part of the discussion so that we may learn from them.)

---

## REVERBERATIONS
### by JayJay Mudridge

I've yet to write about ABA. It's not for lack of effort—as a published poet, my proclivity for floridity and deep appreciation of verbosity is inherent. As an Autist, my communication style hinges most often on directness. This is rarely a dichotomy at odds, save for when I write about Trauma. I recall the psychic gashes and gouges inflicted upon my child-self that reverberate into adulthood still pocking my spiritual skin and leaking ichor behind me decades after the fact, staining my footsteps, restricting my motions . . .

See what I mean? I think it is a way of avoiding stating what has been done to me, a way of disguising the stark reality behind something beautiful. Because, more than anything, I want to believe that beauty can come from pain, that floridity can come from nothingness and verbosity from silence. So, I will do my best to not dress up my experience in prosody. There is power in directness, and so much power has been taken away from me, my inner Autistic light has been so dimmed, my edges so ground down with the rest of me so as to accommodate the neurotypical propensity towards finding differences to be mildly uncomfortable and the impulse to stamp them out at every turn: don't flap, don't rock, don't spin; quiet hands, look me in the eye.

Here is a truth: ABA stole my childhood. The resulting complex post-traumatic stress disorder stole my adulthood. The people who were purported to help me destroyed my life before it even had a chance to begin. Because when you're Autistic like me, your abuse is deemed therapy and it is covered by insurance. The gold standard of "treatment" for a divergent neurology. The first defense against an innocuous, even joyful, difference.

An anecdote, to demonstrate:

In ABA, I was poked and prodded, exposed to sensory stimuli that registered as pain—and still do, to this day—under the pretense that my pain was fear and fear can be eradicated with exposure. When too-loud music was played—or other sensory hell was inflicted, from coating my mouth with honey to push back the times it took me to cry or vomit to not being allowed to use the bathroom unless I endured direct eye contact for minutes on end—to desensitize me, they claimed, as ABA has a fundamental misunderstanding of Autistic neurology, it felt like a roiling on the insides of my neck, climbing my windpipe and spreading into my ear canals, melting my soft tissue as it climbed like ivy up the sides of Usher House. I'd clasp my spindly hands over my ears, shout as the pain seared through my body, claw at my ears and attempt to plug them. My body would rock for comfort, seeking familiarity in the watery motion of the womb, but in ABA comforting movements are not allowed if they are done Autistically: my body was held at the hips to forcibly quell my comfort, my hands held too tightly in my lap by a therapist with pursed lips and furrowed brow.

This, too, registered as pain—unexpected touch, twisting grip, welling tears. Somewhere, a timer beeps, and the music is lowered. This goes on daily, my shrieks and struggles to escape snuffed out like a rain-battered candle by grown-up hands, by exaggerated faces of disapproval or—worse for my six-year-old self—refusal to even acknowledge me, my pain and distress ignored. Though the agony never ceases, I learn to shriek internally, to bite my tongue or cheeks rendering blood if I must in order to avoid any outside signals of pain. My child-self learns that this is how we get Punished—to show distress on the face or body, to show distress Autistically—impotent, inane wailings the cobblestones making up a garden path toward having all I loved taken away for compliance. Don't show it, I learned, and the timer beeps come faster, the music is lowered sooner, the praise too reminiscent of dog training comes, and we move on from this existential dread to the next with only an indifferent data point on a chart marking my perceived progress.

In this way, and all the others, I learned that my body is not my own.

And so, when the therapist's hands clamped down on my hips to pin my twisting form to the floor are replaced by my uncle's hands on my hips; when the hands holding my child-arms still in their enormous, adult hands are replaced by my uncle's hands engulfing my twig-like legs, I do not twist away. There is no thought in my mind, as my uncle's lumbering form slips into the toddler bed I've yet to grow out of like the weight of the whole world, whispering for me to be still and quiet, I believe it to be more of the same. My thoughts were not of the moral wrongness of child molestation, of violation of my body, or breach of my trust. My thoughts were "I need to have quiet hands or I'll be in big trouble," "I need to stay still, or I won't be allowed to eat lunch," "Don't cry, or you won't get to talk about *Star Wars*." These thoughts, and my uncle surreptitiously pressing into my body, are my first formative memories.

---

## ABA in the Past

Before the 1960s, when autism was still poorly understood, some autistic children who showed higher levels of intellect were provided with counseling and talking therapies. On the other end of the scale, those who were showing definite signs of an intellectual disability were often placed in institutional care. Given that so many young children, often incorrectly or unethically, were placed into the care of the state, ABA was a revelation and viewed around the world as wonderfully miraculous.

Early studies that involved the development of ABA focused on rats and a reward-based system that rewarded rats for pushing a bar forward. When the bar was pushed forward, food pellets were released into the cage. The researchers repeated this exercise until the rats got it right. So, the main recognized "therapy" for autistic children was based on a study of rats. Somewhere, somebody came up with the bright idea of using this technique on children so that they would become compliant and do what others wanted them to do.

In 1970, the Young Autism Project at the University of California, Los Angeles, was established with the objective of applying behaviorist methods to children with autism.[7] The project established the methods and goals that grew into ABA. Part of the agenda was to make the child as "normal" as possible by teaching behaviors such as hugging and looking someone in the eye for a sustained period of time. It's important to understand that the term "normal" is different for everyone.

The other focus of the project was on behaviors that are overtly autism-like. Their approach discouraged stimming and often did so with harsh punishment. The therapists on this project slapped, shouted at, or even gave an electrical shock to a child to discourage a specific behavior. The children had to repeat the drills day after day, hour after hour. Videos of these early exercises show therapists holding pieces of food to prompt children to look at them and then rewarding the children with the morsels of food if they made eye contact. It is very hard to believe that this treatment went on, especially as recently as the 1970s. There are academics who deny that various types of abuses took place, but more and more autistic voices are coming forward to say that, during academic studies, they were subjected to violence and inhumane treatment that still affects them.

Of course, many studies done at the time involved violence that resulted in "positive outcomes," meaning that the autistic children became more compliant to the researchers' view of what positive behaviors are in a civilized culture. Each of us has to view this on a personal level, and I look at it this way: If someone wanted me to do something under threat of a cattle prod, I would certainly do it. Pretend someone wanted me to refrain from wearing clothes, which I would want to do in an attempt to be modest. If I did not comply with their choice for me to be naked, I would be met with an electric shock. You know what? I would never wear a stitch of clothing ever again. People do not like pain. Why is that so difficult for people to understand?

Of course, after the study these children were discharged and labeled "fixed." Even though they were supposed to be "fixed" and socially acceptable, children had to undergo follow-up reinforcement programs in the subsequent months and years. The studies started to show that the autistic children were "managing much better," but still not indistin-guishable from their peers. Apparently, many viewed the results as a step in the right direction, because these types of punishment-versus-reward programs continue today in a concerted effort to make autistic people appear "normal."

## ABA and Mike

During one of the virtual visit events I held, an older gentleman asked to speak with me about his own autistic journey. I've identified him as Mike, to protect his privacy. The story that follows is what he related to me during our conversation.

At school, six-year-old Mike found it difficult to remain seated and would click his fingers excessively to the annoyance of his teacher.

Mike's parents were called to the school regarding his behavior and what the next steps to fixing it would entail. These steps were excluding Mike from class activities, shouting at him, and encouraging other children to stay away from him when he was doing non-conforming things. They didn't work. His stims continued both at home and in school. Mike's teacher informed his parents that there were experimental and contemporary methods of therapy that were producing "positive outcomes" for "troubled" children and that they should enroll him.

Following the teacher's advice, Mike's parents enrolled him in a "research group." This "research group" meant that the children would undergo intensive therapy in order to "correct" the behaviors that were causing so much trouble in their lives. While in the research group, Mike made a friend, Henry. Henry was there because his parents didn't like that he refused to eat different foods and refused to play with certain toys. Henry preferred playing with "girls'" toys and didn't have a taste for military figures.

Throughout the research period, Mike was encouraged to stop clicking his fingers; any time he felt the urge to click, a therapist would slap his hand or admonish him in order to remove the urge. If Mike remained in a chair for more than fifteen minutes, he was rewarded with a chocolate treat. He told me that Henry was presented with toys and given a treat when he chose a male action figure over a female action figure.

Over a period of time, under threat of punishment, they both reduced the behaviors that others found troubling. Mike at first felt pleased because he was able to sit for longer periods with his class-mates, and Henry played with more masculine toys. Sadly, when the study finished, the two friends, Mike and Henry, parted ways. Unfortu-nately, years later, Mike developed a fear of moving off a chair when he needed to: he still feared punishment.

Mike recalled being on a date at a cinema and having to use the bathroom during the film. He politely asked his date to be excused. As he was walking through the theater he was filled with a sense of dread that he was doing something wrong. Onlookers troubled him greatly, which often prevented him from going to the cinema and from flying. It wasn't due to a typical fear of flying, but of having to get up out of his seat when the plane was in midair.

In the mid-2000s, Mike was reading more and more material that was demonstrating that children who had undergone such treatment in childhood were coming forward to voice the profound effect that it had upon them. Mike was reading articles from autistic advocates who had to overcome their ABA experiences in the form of counseling and cognitive behavioral therapy (CBT). There was an emerging body of childhood ABA recipients diagnosed with post-traumatic stress disorder (PTSD) in adulthood.

Mike decided that he would undertake a personal mission to locate Henry to discuss the experience that they had together. He put out a social media post in order to find his friend so that they might discuss the experiences they shared in childhood. Mike was very saddened to hear that Henry had taken his own life eighteen years prior.

Mike has spoken about his experience and has endured a typical round of victim blaming, where people accused him of "jumping on the bandwagon" or even straight-up lying! The backlash he has received for telling his story has only added to his stress and deters him from speaking more openly about it.

## Good Now—Bad Later

ABA seems to be much more socially acceptable in the United States even though the basics of it are universal. In the States there are many parents utilizing private practices, and the ones recommended by their insurance provider, for their children. The feedback received from parents who have children undergoing ABA at the present time is generally positive. Parents have reported that their child is managing well and has had a reduction in stimming to the point where they are progressing in the classroom and in family life. Quite often, the command "quiet hands" is used to discourage autistic children from hand flapping. While this can be viewed as teaching children to be polite, it seeks to reduce the aspects of what make autistic children autistic. Given the controversy, some therapists do not use this particular command anymore, but it is still out there in the form of signs in classrooms. The issue with "quiet hands" is that while it is a nonviolent intervention, it still makes a child feel different from everyone else, which reduces their self-confidence. Basically, it shows that their hands are wrong and that everyone else's hands are right!

The best analogy I can equate to ABA is cigarette smoking. One cigarette calms the nerves of the smoker and provides relief from a craving. At that moment one doesn't visualize the harm that cigarettes are causing. Onlookers might say that the person has had a cigarette so they are now calm. In future, when pulmonary disease sets in, it shows that the temporary relief was not worth the long-term pain.

Many autistic advocates share this view. ABA can demonstrate positive changes at that moment. However, in an autistic person's future, the potential development or worsening of existing mental health issues is of grave concern. Long-term participation in what is, in essence, a compliance therapy can greatly reduce the self-esteem of autistic people. Many autistic people report that they live in fear that they are not doing what is expected of them. When someone spends a prolonged period having to get the approval of a therapist for "normal" behavior, they will undoubtedly learn that approval is always required.

A lot of studies promote the efficacy of ABA. There exist scholarly articles and studies to show how ABA is "working." Technically, this isn't a lie, but rather it's hiding the consequences that may appear in later life. ABA is based on quantitative research, not qualitative research. Success is measured in the moment rather than viewing the total long-term consequences on the whole person. It will be very interesting to see how the ABA success stories involving children in 2020 will differ in the year 2050. I would imagine that in thirty years there might be a lot of autistic children who grew to be autistic adults who are very reliant on someone else for approval.

## Acceptance Therapies

Luckily, I wasn't a victim of any institutional or medical abuse when I was younger. In the 1990s, the topic of autism was much more mainstream and attitudes toward autistic children were shifting to a more positive tone. That brought about some therapies that don't attempt to "change" autistic people. When I was young, I wanted to be like everyone else. When I started cognitive behavioral therapy (CBT) and psychotherapy, I relayed this to the therapists. Frankly, if I hadn't had personal positive experiences, I wouldn't be the proud autistic person that I am today.

When I told my story to the various therapists I worked with over the years, they were quick to inform me that they wouldn't be able to change me, nor did they want to even try. This was a breath of fresh air. I had felt that I needed to be like everybody else to fit in, and they allowed me to be me. It only takes some very limited research to realize that the general view is that autism is a detriment and that we need a lot of additional help to become productive and meaningful members of the "normal" society around us.

Therapies that promote acceptance, self-healing, and forgiveness of self seem to be received with much more positivity within the autistic community. In my view, all therapies should be centered on this notion. Not just for autistics, but for everyone. Acceptance of each other should be everyone's goal. To be able to accept yourself and have others accept you in return would make the world a much happier place in which to live.

## Cognitive Behavioral Therapy (CBT)

CBT is designed to help people notice and understand how their thoughts, behaviors, and emotions affect each other. It is also designed to help them learn new ways of thinking about and responding to distressing situations. This often involves looking at their childhood and other stressful events through adult eyes. The human bias often restricts the desire to look at past experiences with objectivity.

The therapist breaks down problems into feelings, thoughts, and actions that are unhelpful or unrealistic. Then the therapist teaches the client how to replace those feelings, thoughts, and actions with more helpful and realistic ones. That process helps one understand how they can approach and work out a situation. In my case, I always viewed myself as an outsider who had many difficulties in school and as a young man. I believed myself to be a man who would never really fit anywhere and would have to sit quietly while society passed me by until it was my time to go.

CBT allowed me to face the fears that I had, many of which were unintentionally self-inflicted. Along the way, I had gained a persecution complex even though my parents, teachers, and friends all wanted only what was best for me. As a young adult, I was, like many people, naturally defensive when I felt I was being criticized. My relentless desire to prove people wrong was consuming my entire life and destroying the relationship I was trying to build with my infant son. Some people have said that I am a bit of a dreamer, and my dreams haven't ceased. Nor have I become totally at one with reality, but I no longer chase my dreams with the attitude of giving people who doubted me the middle finger. I chase them because they are goals that I have set for myself. I have found that chasing achievement and self-satisfaction are much more valuable than chasing approval.

I voiced my dislike of having had a classroom assistant throughout my school days and how it was a system that made me stand out from everyone else and made me feel different. I had a rejection complex because I went to different playgroups than many of the other children. That added to an irrational fear of being rejected or unwanted. CBT helped me change my thinking so that I now feel that, instead of life giving me one obstacle after another, my life has been one victory after another to get to the stage where I am now. Many autistic people go through CBT in adulthood and it is being tried on younger children, too. Opinions to date are quite mixed, and research continues.

Of course CBT, like any therapy, isn't best for every single person, and there are some autistic voices that oppose it. I can only report that my own experience was generally positive, and when people voice a concern to me, I research further. Not in an academic way where I create trials, peer-reviewed papers, or laboratory research, but by simply researching what others say and any clinical findings that may be available.

To date, I haven't found anything specifically designed to oppose CBT, and no group has appealed for a ban of CBT. The reverse is true of ABA, where there are many hundreds of statements on social media and online that are actively campaigning for ABA to be outlawed. I make no secret of the fact that I am a mere layman, but no matter who you are, this should provoke serious thought.

## Why Is It Up to Us to Change?

In my view, this is the main issue: Why does it have to be the autistic community that has to change? There are things I do that are not viewed as normal by everyone else. Yet, in the perspective of some individuals and groups, it is I who must change. Some teachers and employers do not understand autistic people around them and, therefore, believe we are the ones who have to change.

It is very clear that autistic people are autistic for their entire lives. Everyone else can be taught to be more accepting of us. They can surpass ignorance in a way that we cannot stop being autistic. It all stems from the connotation of "normal." Generally, that term is defined by what the majority does and believes is the hypothetical blueprint in which all sections of society must fit.

I needed therapy; however, I am not an advocate who will say that no autistic person ever needs therapy and everyone should just accept us and that is the end of it. If I continued to hold the belief that I was being persecuted and that I was, in the eyes of others and myself, subhuman, I couldn't imagine the dark path my life would have taken. I have refused help and support and sometimes didn't realize I needed it when I actually did need it and benefited from it! I would encourage everyone who holds any self-hatred, or who doesn't view being autistic as a wonderful thing, to find the assistance that will help you remedy these things. I know that many will read this book and still use the word "autism" to define an intellectual disability. Those who are autistic with an accompanying intellectual disability will need much more help and support in childhood, and that is okay too. The significance of support should be to help you find your value and appreciate that.

Like countless others in the autistic community, there were times in my life when I believed that I needed to be fixed. I believed those people who said I should be just like them if I were to accomplish anything. I didn't know about neurodiversity and acceptance until relatively recently. But I was fortunate. At no time or stage in my life did my parents want me to change. It took time for me to realize that my personal desire to hide being autistic was not the fault of my parents or anyone else; it was only my fault for not accepting myself.

Autistic people are among the most studied people in the world. I went through innumerable evaluations, appointments, assessments, and reviews. I have no doubt that these were all done to support me and make sure that everyone involved with me could bring out the best in me. Throughout my youth, there seemed to be an underlying, silent notion that I had absolutely no idea what direction my life would take and that I needed support in finding a way.

The truth is, my desire to succeed was already there. I wanted to go to university; I wanted to do well at school—and I did. In the eyes of my schools, and everyone who helped me, I am a success story. I did very well academically; I passed every exam without having to repeat any, and I eventually went on to become a university graduate. I knew what I wanted to do, I knew where I wanted to go, and I knew that the fuss around me was not always warranted. I did pick up a lot of useful information and tips that helped me study and communicate, but I often think that this would have happened anyway.

Undergoing so many interventions made me feel like I was a broken outsider. Nobody else around me was getting the attention that I was getting. I realize now that the extra attention around me could have had a negative effect on others around me. My perception at the time was that I wasn't worth associating with, which is why I had people assigned to assist me. In hindsight, I am thankful for the support I received from many hearts that were in the right place, but that didn't stop me from carrying scars that deeply affected me into adulthood.

Diane McGarvey shared a wonderful example of how therapies are changing. After following the guidelines of autism spectrum disorder (ASD) training, she saw no difference in her child. ASD training uses rewards linked to goals, but after attending one of my training sessions, she started interacting with her daughter in a very different way, which she describes below.

---

## THE POWER OF POSITIVITY
### *by* **Diane McGarvey**

My eldest of four daughters was diagnosed with autism when she began primary school at six. I was always concerned about her high levels of anxiety and having very basic knowledge of autism, I therefore didn't suspect that she would have autism; rather that she was and still remains a highly anxious child. My poor knowledge of autism consisted of assuming children would have behavior issues, have no eye contact, and have difficulties communicating. This wasn't my child. She was intelligent, witty, enjoyed the company of others, held excellent eye contact, but was highly anxious. Don't get me wrong—there was always a tantrum getting dressed in the morning, picking out clothes to wear, or when her siblings were receiving more attention than she was (in her eyes); however, all toddlers and young children go through these stages, don't they?

However, as her anxiety worsened when she began school, I sought some help for her. Teachers couldn't believe it when I informed them of how anxious she was outside of school, as she was calm and happy in school. Later I discovered this is the classic masking that is referred to, particularly with girls who have autism. When she was finally diagnosed with autism, again the teachers were quite shocked.

As part of her ASD support plan, my husband and I attended autism awareness training and also training on strategies used to support children with autism. I have used endless reward charts, sticker charts, and tokens for efforts made when she managed to achieve something that she wouldn't normally do due to anxiety. However, things went from bad to worse. COVID happened and schools closed at the time that was most important to her, transitioning to secondary school. No final seventh grade goodbyes, no end-of-the-year trip, no visits to secondary schools—everything was put on hold. For a child who has developed separation anxiety towards her mother over the years, this negative move into lockdown became a positive move for her as she soon realized that she and I could be together every day. I worked from home, my exercise class had stopped, I couldn't attend social events with friends—all of which she'd previously struggled with.

School reopened and, amazingly, she attended her new school without any fear. However, the fear lies with events that will never happen rather than her being able to channel real fears, like starting a new school. My daughter now believes that every time I leave our home I will never return—that I will die, or just decide that I won't come home and live with someone else. She even goes so far as to believe I would live on the streets rather than return home to her. She is a child that is loved dearly by her entire family. She has never experienced any trauma, has never had a close relation who has passed away, and, as part of my strategy to alleviate her anxieties, I have always provided her with a detailed plan of my movements when I need to leave the house for work.

ASD (autism spectrum disorder) training informs us to apply rewards linked to goals that she needs to achieve. I have completed daily journals with her based on emotional regulation and set goals with rewards attached, yet there was no change.

Then I attended Jude's training and realized very quickly that I wasn't helping my child at all. Jude really encouraged his participants to consider our children's positive behaviors. He also got me thinking: Had I really asked my child what I could do for her, or have all the strategies I have implemented been based on what I want for her? Jude made me realize that reward charts are putting a floodlight on her inadequacies. After living in such a negative environment, I nearly forgot about the amazing personality traits that my child has. I asked her what I could do to help. She wanted me to sleep beside her at night, as she was frightened. She wanted me to not attend my exercise class for a little while so she can get used to me going to work first.

All very sensible things that I thought would only create dependency rather than lead to independence.

As we battle on with managing her extreme fears, that by no means are leaving her any time soon, I constantly hear Jude's voice in my ear saying "Just ask what is wrong?" and "Accept everything about your child; always remembering the positives." This has helped me no end.

---

## Changing the Framework

The notion that autistic children all have to undergo extensive therapy is a generalization that doesn't sit well with many in the autistic community. The current framework seems to be that a diagnosis automatically leads to a referral for therapy that often exceeds thirty hours per week, per child. This type of diagnosis seems to come more from the medical community and, frankly, concerned parents will usually follow the advice of their doctor without exploring other options. I think most doctors have a serious desire to help our community, but the treatments they prescribe need to include emotional support that we are who we are and that it is fine to be who we are.

The first place I feel this should be addressed is in medical schools. The educational platform seems to be that autistic children are in need of being "normalized." When it comes to autistic children, would it not be more beneficial for parents to have training and support to accept their autistic children? That type of training would involve understanding what being autistic really means to the autistic person and that the risk of changing or minimizing often-harmless traits like stimming could have an adverse effect in adulthood. Of course, this doesn't and won't happen in every case, although there is a risk that it can. It's like cigarette smoking: not every person will get lung cancer, although the risk is definitely there.

There are harmful stims like head banging or incessant scratching that certainly demand some type of intervention, especially in much younger children. The main point remains the same: stims, whether positive or negative, are an emotional response that may be brought on by frustration, sadness, or even happiness.

I have often asked teachers to really examine the reason why stimming in a classroom causes so much discomfort. Many will reply that some stims can be distracting and disruptive to other pupils within their classroom. Are they really? Are other children to blame, or is it more distracting for the teacher than it is for the other pupils in the classroom? The jury seems to be out on this one, although it is a very interesting thought.

I met one teacher who had an autistic child at home and another in her classroom. Given her personal life experience, she knew that her son's stimming was harmless and didn't overly distract other family members at home. When the autistic boy in her classroom tapped his feet on the floor, she chose to allow him to do this freely. Over time, her pupil's stims were normalized within the classroom and the other children naturally accepted him without any need to admonish or highlight the stims to the class.

This was a very promising discovery, if one could call it that. The other pupils in the classroom accepted the tolerance displayed by the teacher. This is just one example of a harmless stim, though if stims or other behaviors involved harm to the pupil or others, it would be an entirely different story.

My denial of the fact that I was autistic was a defense mechanism that sheltered me from pain. As human beings, denial can be a necessity, especially when we are not mentally or emotionally strong enough to deal with a particular situation. I'm sure that somewhere along the journey, denial has served me well. I know it did when I was training to become a social worker. I didn't allow what I viewed at the time as a limitation to stop me from achieving my goals. I still do this, although with a higher sense of pride than in the past.

I still use my thought processes as a force for good. I haven't completely dropped my way of thinking in order to replace it with a new one; I simply use it more effectively. I don't do small talk in the same way I don't do light reading. I may not understand society, culture, or human nature as much as the next person, but that doesn't stop me from trying to interpret things in my own way.

One of my favorite books is Friedrich Nietzsche's classic *Thus Spoke Zarathustra*. It's the story of the travels of an ancient prophet and the lessons he provides to strangers along the way. I pick up this book at least once a year as it gives deep analogies on the simple things in life that sometimes pass me by. On one of his journeys, Zarathustra encountered a small boy staring out across the valley as he rested against a tree. In a discussion about strength and power, Zarathustra explained that he couldn't shake the tree and tip it over, no matter how hard he tried. Zarathustra, who viewed himself as a physically strong man, could not budge the tree. Then he told the boy that even though he couldn't move the tree, a powerful but invisible wind could topple the tree given a forceful gust of unseen energy.

I understood the concept this way: in the literal sense, the wind is much stronger than any one individual. It's an obvious, and somewhat tedious, observation that the wind could blow a tree down much quicker than a man would be able to push it over. I tried to go slightly deeper while understanding that the invisible forces, in a literal sense, are gravity or the physical force of a gale knocking the tree over.

I recently read this book again, and the beauty of the philosophy is that it can be interpreted on a much deeper level than when I initially read it, which is likely due to the acquisition of wisdom that comes with age. After my last reading, I viewed the invisible force as anger, sadness, discrimination, and prejudice. These are the invisible forces that ride and circulate in the wind and can cause us, the trees, the autistic community, to fall.

When I reached that deeper conclusion, a thought occurred to me. We need to become the powerful invisible force. Not in a militant way or a way that tramples over the rights and feelings of others, but to perpetuate a valid foundational acceptance that autistic people are here and here to stay! For me, that was quite profound.

I once believed that we needed to be trees that were so strong that they could never be felled. Building resilience is one thing, but not having to withstand the invisible force of judgment provides a much better prospect for our overall success.

There's a huge difference between physical strength and an invisible force. Some of the worst forces in the world can be invisible. Discrimination, anger, ignorance, and greed are all invisible. They may not be seen, but they exist. They are there, causing destruction. However, if autistic people are the tree, and if the tree was, in some way, protected from the discriminatory philosophical wind, it wouldn't blow down so easily. In the past, I was easily blown down. The slightest hiccup or breath of wind in my life would have felled me immediately. When I knew the wind was coming, I learned how to brace myself—and I still do, but I shouldn't have to anymore. None of us should have to brace ourselves against invisible forces of destruction.

# 9

# Higher Education

Personally, I love to plan. So, with my deep love of planning, I decided to prepare to attend university. By midsummer, I learned that I had the grades to get into the social work degree program that I had applied for and that I would be attending the Ulster University at Magee Campus in Ireland. The seven years of secondary education seemed to pass by so quickly, even though when I was there, I thought it was never going to end. Even my parents agreed with me on this point, even though they had to endure my incessant ramblings about how miserable I was for the entire time I was there.

This step of pursuing my goal to get a higher education was incredibly daunting, as I tend to feel change much more acutely than other people. I'd had a childhood full of communication difficulties, mainly because people did not understand my methods of communicating; I couldn't seem to get my point of view understood, which prompted a disinterest in connecting with other people. It's actually quite ironic that I decided to become a social worker! I recently realized that many autistic people have had a similar experience. School does not last forever and, at some point, we must join the responsible workforce of society, autism or not!

Selecting a career in psychology let Alex Pearson learn about others and more about herself. She not only completed the original classes but also went on to graduate studies. One of the things that she addressed with me was how many of us in the community camouflage or mask in order to hide who we truly are. Here's her story of the value of removing the mask:

---

## LIFE AFTER THE MASK
### by **Alex Pearson**

Camouflaging is a method for suppressing autistic traits, which is an umbrella term that includes masking (i.e., taking on neurotypical traits as your own), assimilation (i.e., trying to fit in with everyone else so people don't notice you are different), and compensation (i.e., finding ways around things that are naturally difficult), which I only discovered at the age of twenty-five, following learning that I am autistic coupled with completing six years of higher education in psychology. I entered the field of psychology because of two things: (1) I felt drawn to individuals who were different—had been through some type of trauma—and I felt like I understood certain people on a different level (what I now know to be neurodiverse individuals), and (2) we often engaged in family therapy, and I noted in these conversations I was always diagnosing the problems in terms of behaviors, cognitions, and attitudes. I was always very objective in my assessments, and even our family therapist mentioned that I could have led our sessions. I didn't realize at the time that I had entered the field to understand myself better and to find answers about how humans operate. Psychology unlocked hundreds of frameworks to explain the world, why people do the things they do, think the things they think, and engage in the strange social behaviors/norms that often arise in groups. This provided me with language to even better describe and frame up my "informal social science" work I had been doing for twenty years prior.

During my graduate studies in industrial/organizational psychology (i.e., the employee-centered studies of how to make work better, how to build, deliver, and measure training curriculum, and how to make selection systems/performance appraisals more fair) I learned about the emerging work large corporations were engaged in concerning neurodiversity. I attended a panel on the subject where Tim Goldstein presented along with executives from JPMorgan Chase and SAP. Thereafter, I found the organization "Potentia" on LinkedIn and cold-messaged my now-CEO and direct boss, Jeff Miller. I shared with him my passions in the area, my work with autism studies in college, and that my greatest dream would be to consult with organizations on inclusion by way of reworking current systems (like the selection process) and training companies on the brilliance and worthiness of neurodiverse minds to rewrite a highly stigmatized narrative. Jeff urged me to meet Shawn Fry, Potentia's chief innovation officer, prior to my hire, and while we were only supposed to meet for a quick thirty minutes, we spoke for three hours about our skills/abilities, our visions for the future, and the stories of our past. We both cried and connected deeply, and soon after I learned that the ease of our friendship development and comfort in interactions is because we are both autistic. Without Shawn, I would have never learned who I am. I would have never been able to write this piece and share with you an analysis of my life before I knew. I spent months weeping and grieving over my past self, who tried so desperately (and at the expense of mental health and feelings of self-worth) to be neurotypical, when in fact my neurodiverse self is MUCH more fascinating, smart, fun, silly, raw, and honest. Learning how to love myself has been so rewarding. I am proud to speak about my experience and my approach to the world being neurodiverse through my stories and social media posts. I have chosen to dedicate the rest of my life to advocacy for the autistic community . . . for strong and safe friendships, loving relationships, comfortable workplace environments, and our own feelings of self-efficacy and empowerment. I especially want to dedicate substantial effort to helping women who are autistic discover themselves and learn that there are people JUST like them who will love and welcome their authenticity.

"MASK OFF!"

---

I often think about how removing the mask that we use to make us appear more uniform would change the university experience for autistic students. One way that I used to mask was research. If I knew my surroundings, even the history surrounding them, I was more comfortable. So, I set about educating myself about the place of my education.

## Before Attending University

Even though at this stage I did not fully accept and embrace the fact I was autistic, my mind came up with a wonderful idea. In order to not fear the environment that I was going into, I decided to research the university itself. I got a map of the campus online as well as the old building plans for it. I researched the entire history of the school so that I became acquainted with it. I learned that in the 1860s it was a theology school, which made sense to me because of the style of architecture of the main building on the campus.

I read my course notes and my class timetables and mapped out every class. I knew exactly where I had to go and how to get there utilizing the vast array of entrances into and out of the campus. At the time, there were rumors circulating that the school had a secret underground control room dating back to a time when the Royal Navy used the building during World War II. This tale of clandestine intrigue completely captured my imagination and added a sense of mystery, which I found fascinating. For anyone going to a new school, I highly recommend researching the school or workplace you will be attending. It certainly helped me avoid an overwhelming first day on campus.

Almost every college will list the course staff for each subject taught that one can study. I looked up the profiles for every professor I would have. The fact that I have some difficulty putting a face to a name causes me some discomfort, even today. I have an irrational fear of knowing somebody's name and then having to meet them without knowing exactly what they look like. Preparation is key for almost anything in life, and doing preliminary research certainly helped ease my own first-day anxieties. By the time I had started in September 2009, I knew all my professors from their profiles and I knew all of the buildings so well that I probably could have gone from class to class blindfolded. It may sound like a lot of diligent work, but knowing as much as I possibly could, about a new experience and place, certainly helped me get off on the right foot.

# First Day

I arrived at the campus and I felt as if I had been there forever! I knew every nook and cranny of the campus, despite not needing to know it all. The only thing I wasn't, and couldn't be, prepared for was meeting the classmates I would be studying with for the next three years. I don't "mingle" with others very well, and I don't easily introduce myself in a new or unscripted situation. That is gradually changing. Since graduating, I have met and tutored social work students during their working placements. This course seemed to attract a disproportionate number of mature students compared to other courses. Most of my classmates were mature students and that was okay with me; at that time, I tended to form relationships much better with older people than those my own age or younger. Numerous autistic people I have spoken with seem to experience similar interpersonal relationships. As a child, I spent more time with a classroom assistant and one-on-one with teachers than mixing with other children my age. Being able to comfortably create friendships and relationships with older adults seems to be a common theme among the autistic community, and the attention we receive as children from adults could be part of the reason we respond this way.

University or any third-level education places a large emphasis on independent learning and study. Leaving the organized structure of secondary school was an exceedingly difficult thing to adapt to. I was used to receiving a timetable, filling my days with everything from what time I went into school in the morning through the entire day. My new timetable had many gaps in it. There were lectures and seminars dotted here and there throughout the week, but the rest was just blank! My day felt hollow and disjointed and the spaces between courses and lectures left me sitting alone, feeling scattered and unfocused.

## Coping with Independent Study

I didn't know how the structure of third-level education would work, and it troubled me greatly. I sat at home wondering what I should do in the gaps of time between courses. The words "independent study" could mean anything! I was always interested in studying subjects that most appealed to me at any specific time. For the first few weeks, I didn't really know what to do between my lectures and seminars, so I would go home without visiting the library or getting to know my classmates.

Also, I wasn't used to sitting in a classroom by myself without a classroom assistant. That was a huge leap for me. It was a change but, since third-level education is entirely voluntary, the responsibility of care for certain students is less than it is in compulsory education classes. On reflection, I certainly believe that the gradual withdrawal of classroom assistance in the final year of an autistic child's secondary education would be of great benefit to the student. If an autistic child learns a trade or goes to college, the same level of support simply isn't provided, unless they seek it through student groups or a course tutor. Everyone was assigned a course tutor whom we could have one-on-one time with. This normally happened a couple of times a month, and I knew I had to try to take advantage of it.

As a young man, I was never open with others about being autistic. I had to decide if I would tell my course tutor that I was autistic. I was initially very hesitant, as I had never declared it before to anyone who wasn't a family member or remarkably close friend. I held the same fear that many in the autistic community have, and that was the fear of being judged by others when I declared that I was autistic. Somehow, I irrationally believed that this might place me under closer supervision or surveillance of some kind. I decided that disclosing my autism to my course tutor was the best course of action. When I did, the sense of relief that came to me was unimaginably immense!

My course tutor was incredibly understanding. I spoke openly about my concern of being guided through my education and explained that I wanted to basically do as much as I could myself. I discussed my worries about "independent study" and what it meant. Together, we worked on a study timetable regarding each of the classes I was taking. I allocated time to read the course materials and study them in the library. I took control of my own studies and preparation for examinations and assignments.

I was able to write out which course materials were assigned in each class and allocate specific times to read them. I found myself able to learn the material very easily when I had a set structure in place, and I kept up this routine for my entire three years at the school! This was the first substantial indication that my thirst for routine and order was to my advantage, but only in the learning environment.

Many would view an emphasis on order and routine as a deficit; I turned the so-called deficit into a working advantage. My routine meant that I spent many hours in the library reading the books that were important to my studies, and that practice helped me greatly, even though I designed it myself.

I can't provide an exact method of how every autistic student can study, although one nugget of gold remains the same for everyone: don't be afraid to ask for guidance and support. If I hadn't reached out for support and guidance, I probably wouldn't have graduated or have the social work job I have now! This is how I managed for three years, and it served me incredibly well. With a clear vision of how to proceed and succeed, I was able to do what needed to be done.

## Socializing at the University

The university experience always brings up questions when I meet autistic teens or the parents of autistic kids. The most common curiosity is the delicate topic of making friends. Many teens are worried about how they are going to interact or mix in with the new environment. The teachings of Freud address the fact that as humans, we are social beings; to a large extent, I agree that is true.

So many parents ask me, "My child doesn't make any friends. How can they be better at it?"

This is a question that conjures up personal emotions on so many levels. I remember teachers and classroom assistants, with their hearts in the right place, trying to encourage me to mix with other people when I clearly didn't wish to. A common theme of the autistic existence is feeling pressured to behave like other children who are not autistic. It is an accepted myth that autistic people are loners and incapable of making friends. Many people, autistic or not, love their own company, including me!

Some of the most distressing times for me as a child, and even as an adult, were when people *made* me socialize. Human interaction is important, but I always did this in my own time. Being autistic isn't the reason why I am a bit of a cynic; I blame that on the fact that I'm a social worker. Working in a career that deals with so much abuse, poverty, and lack of equality did that to me! But I am not cynical about everything.

When I meet a group of autistic teens and young adults, we usually forge a deep connection and bond over the fact that we don't like people very much and actually prefer our own company. One of the greatest ironies of my life is that I make friends over the topic of not making friends. We all laugh and joke about being a group of people who don't like being in groups. Yes, we autistic people can joke and have a sense of humor too! I honestly can't recall a time in my life when I laughed as much as I do now.

Still, it is quite sad that many autistic teens are worried about communal encounters after leaving school. The social etiquette expectation that everyone must flock together is a very daunting prospect and a question I certainly would have asked if there was an autistic adult to ask questions of when I was young.

Many parents and professionals believe that when an autistic child or adult doesn't make friends, it is because we simply can't. That just isn't true. I didn't always want to mix or complete group tasks if I didn't have to. I have also met autistic people who have many friends and are extremely popular in their own social circles. Some psychological studies and advocacy groups are starting to gather evidence that encouraging or forcing autistic children to socialize can be more harmful than having a large social circle. Depending on what the autistic person's special interests are, they can and do meet other people! As a participant in enthusiast social media pages, I have met others like me. I believe that encouraging special interest groups is a great way to meet and have conversations with other like-minded people! This is not just advice for autistic people, because it can apply to anybody.

Universities always have extracurricular activities and interest clubs. My school had an astronomy club. I was skeptical about joining because of the high volume of clouds and rain that hang over the Emerald Isle; it's hard to stargaze when you can't see the stars because it's a rainy night. I joined anyway. There are extracurricular clubs that welcome everyone with open arms, so I recommend that you check them out before you enroll in school.

Imagine, if you will, that I ask you to join one of the *Titanic* enthusiasts' groups that I belong to. You may have absolutely no knowledge or interest in the topic whatsoever. If I were to say to you that your lack of interest in the *Titanic* is greatly troubling to society and you need help, you would look at me with squinted eyes and a tilted head. Why should that standard be different for autistic people? If we don't want to mix and congregate, we are labeled "weird," but if a non-autistic person doesn't want to mix, they are simply disinterested in the subject and that's okay. This is an inequality that everyone should thoughtfully consider. We need to retrain our thinking so that we treat each other equally, without labels.

Making friends at the university wasn't as difficult for me as I thought it might be. The majority were mature students, and the younger members of the class naturally flocked together. Because I had my own special interests and way of being, I didn't integrate well at school. That didn't really bother me at all for the most part, but I realized something when I left school: everyone in my class had the same goal. They wanted to become qualified social workers.

Secondary schools are a melting pot of people, all with their own individual ideas and paths in life. Many go on to be dentists, doctors, factory workers, hairdressers, and so on. Everyone is unique in the path they want their life to take, and that can make it much harder to fit in and find people with similar goals or interests as you. Therefore, I thought I didn't really fit in well. I found it hard to meet people with similar goals in life. In my class, no one knew that my goal was to go into social work.

At the university, I found it easy to integrate—much easier than I'd ever believed, because I had never been in an environment that allowed me to share the same interest as others. I wasn't a huge fan of group tasks at school, but at the university I enjoyed collaborating with other people. I was even able to show off my organizational skills to everyone without feeling the need to take charge. On one occasion, I had to give a presentation to my class on a poster that our group had made that highlighted the issue of domestic violence. I rehearsed my speech many times in the library and sneaked into the lecture hall so I could accomplish my pre-presentation ritual. It helps me when I know the environment of everything I do in life—at least, as much as I can.

I had participated in school plays and, using the skills I'd learned there, I was able to confidently and competently present our group's ideas to the class. That's when I realized that I was quite good at public speaking. When I walked around the space at the front of the lecture hall with my microphone, my course tutor—who also happened to be the examiner—gave me a look of surprise and professional pride. This was someone I had confided in because I knew I wasn't like my classmates. She knew I could do it, and boy did I! When I looked across the hall at my classmates, they were nodding and smiling as I was speaking. I couldn't believe it!

## Discover What You Do Well

When I identified what my strengths were, I focused much less on what society would view as my weaknesses. Yes, my attention span is short, my small-talk skills aren't wonderful, and I can lose track of time when I am hyper-focused. But when I realized what I was good at and built self-confidence around that, I focused my energy on those things. In my case, I concentrated on verbal presentations and written assignments. I always found examinations difficult because I am easily distracted, but I learned that if I just look at the paper and nothing else, I get by.

My course, as is true of many, wasn't entirely classroom based. Instead of looking at the course one year at a time, I looked at the entire length of the course. Like all health and social care degrees, I also had work placements. For a degree in social work, there were two eighteen-week placements during the second and third years. One was focused on working with children in need and the other on adults who had mental health issues, had learning disabilities, or were elderly. The only problem I had was that I didn't find out where I was going until two weeks prior to beginning the work placement.

I was prepared when the board made the announcement; I took all the details down and made sure that I was able to meet the team and the supervisor prior to beginning work. I thought that I had come up with the genius idea of getting acquainted with my colleagues and environment prior to the placement starting, but this was already encouraged and expected by the faculty staff. Even when my environment changed, I was hesitant to tell my colleagues about being autistic. I didn't do this for my first placement, and I found it quite hard. I had a certain way of working, writing things down and organizing my days. When it came to working life, my day was easily interrupted by having to shadow a colleague during an emergency child protection call. While training for the responsibilities I would have to carry out in working life, it wasn't as easy to plan my days as effectively as I had when I was classroom based.

The first time my schedule was interrupted came as a complete shock. I had decided to dedicate my morning to writing reports of the home visits I had carried out the previous day. I was sitting there with my notepad, my pen, my laptop, and a checklist of all I had to accomplish when a colleague burst through my door. The police had flagged an emergency child protection situation and the social worker wanted to take me with her to learn and observe. Although I knew that this would be part of my course, having to abandon my plan still caused slight discomfort for me. To some this may sound very childish, but the possibility that my plans might have to change was something I had to learn, and learn fast! Today, I can deal with emergency concerns as they happen because I know it is part of my profession and I have learned to be more flexible with my plans.

This experience opened my eyes in other ways, too. It was clear that the child we went to see was a victim of horrible physical abuse. I was only twenty years old and facing a harrowing scene. I saw first-hand the reality of some of the darkest corners of our society, corners that I thought only existed in fiction. Was I selfish? Was I too reliant on control? Perhaps, to a degree, I was. Clichés are clichés for a reason, and I learned that one is entirely true: you should always expect the unexpected, no matter your course of study or trade. If I had decided to become a nurse, I couldn't disregard a patient that came into the emergency room riddled with bullets simply because I had something else planned for that morning.

Studying to become a social worker awakened me to many of the unseemly realities of life. When I learned of the oppressions that many people and communities face, I realized that I was somewhat oppressed myself. I heard so many perspectives from those who had physical disabilities, had learning disabilities, and were survivors of abuse. The common theme that runs through all their stories is that these groups are identified by many misconceptions and their voices are greatly underrepresented. Generally, their education had been focused solely around the challenges that those who are marginalized experience. Being autistic, I genuinely identified with this.

Every week we would have someone come from each service user group to discuss their personal experience and expertise. One day, an "autism expert" came to speak to our class. I looked forward to hearing what he had to say about the topic, since I was personally involved at a much more real level than my classmates or professors. One slide that the expert showed said that autistic people could lack empathy. Nobody in my class knew that I was autistic; the expert certainly did not know that his words and judgment were directed at me and people like me. Seeing somebody stand there and teach a room full of professionals about the negative views on autism saddened me. I felt quite ashamed and didn't really know where to look or how to react.

Then suddenly, I felt my hand leave my side, my mouth opened, and I challenged the slide that he had put up. I asked him to imagine an autistic person hearing such an unkind thing from someone they did not even know. This is what I had been subjected to my entire life. People viewed me differently and focused on the negative stereotypes applied to autism rather than what I could and had accomplished. I questioned *his* empathy level by showing these slides without knowing if people in the room had any personal connection to autism. With a wry smile, he conceded that this was a particularly good point and moved on with the rest of his presentation.

I didn't realize this at the time, but this was probably my first moment of advocating for myself and, by default, autistic people everywhere. Even though I didn't like that I was autistic at the time, I was beginning to understand why I'd held a self-hatred for so many years. I didn't accept it and love it like I do now. But, back then, these misconceptions are what my parents were told about me. This is what my teachers were told about me. This is the societal view of what autism is. Is it any wonder that so many autistic people have so many identity crises and low self-esteem? We were only one group that heard that presentation. How many others had heard the expert and his negative characterizations of autistic people?

His presentation about autistic people also discussed their love of order, their obsessive behaviors, and that they don't generally mix well in social settings. These "traits" are only measured from the neurotypical standpoint. Apparently, the reason I am not like everyone else is because the majority determines what "normal" is, and how far you stray from that determines if you are autistic or not.

It's true; a sense of order and routine is something I love. It is a common theme in the autistic community and one that is often misunderstood. If you look up the dictionary definition of "autistic," you will read something like this: *Autism is a neurodevelopmental disorder characterized by obsessive and repetitive patterns of behavior and interests.*

That definition upsets me greatly. To me it poses more questions than answers. In the eyes of others, the definition is a limitation that boxes in people like me. My entire existence as an autistic person characterized by one derogatory sentence with a structure of demeaning words. It tells me that if you are autistic, there is not much good about you.

Even when participating in a course that teaches about anti-oppression and nonjudgmental attitudes, there were still some there. In the big, bad, and unfortunately real world, there is still a lack of understanding and acceptance for autistic people. As hard as that may be to read or hear, it was a truth that faced me as I listened to that presentation. Although I love being prepared, I had to learn to expect the unexpected. Being prepared for a possible sudden alteration to my day's schedule is something that has taken me years to master, and working on being more flexible when I was at university certainly helped me. We all, neurotypical and neurodiverse, have to change a little to work together to make things better.

That was a learning and growth journey for sure! I graduated in July 2012 as a fully-fledged social worker. Imagine! The guy who talks about all his "social difficulties" became a social worker and does it every day of his life. I strutted across the stage at the graduation ceremony and waved to my parents, who have been in my corner every step of the way. They knew I could do it long before I even knew that I could!

I was blessed to have amazing teachers throughout my time there. Despite being one of the youngest in the class, I managed to get through the entire course. Many parts of it weren't easy, but I don't believe any student experience is. Learning to adapt to new situations is what helped me most throughout this time. It was totally different than what I was used to, and my expectations were different than what the experience was actually like.

For any autistic student about to embark on the university journey, do not fear the social aspect. Everyone is there for the same reason: to pass the course. It really isn't as much of a competition or popularity contest as might be experienced in secondary school. When I was in secondary school, I was somewhat the class clown. I still am, although I don't get in trouble for it anymore. When you leave school, the possibilities are endless. You can apply yourself to training colleges, universities, and work environments, whatever you choose. All that you learn contributes to your life.

Telling my course tutor that I was autistic was the best thing that I did. I am, by nature, an enormously proud person and it took a lot out of me to ask for help. Had I not told her I was autistic, I may not have had the guidance that helped me through the entire course. Once I understood the value of that communication, I was happy to receive advice on how to structure and tailor my own student experience.

## Valuable Advice

Having successfully completed the course, I was given another piece of amazing advice that every single professional should note. My tutor called me into her office before graduation. I knew that I had passed the course and would receive my degree the following month. She was very understanding and told me to use the wonderful way my mind is programmed to help others.

What other people might see as my limitations could be turned to my advantage. My attention to detail has helped me spot subtle signs of abuse. My logical and methodical way of working has helped me to take a step back, analyze a situation, and decide on a safe way forward in the event of a crisis. Those are attributes that can and have helped other people, just as she suggested.

The possibilities are endless when you leave school. I share this advice with everyone on the spectrum: no matter what career path you select, know that autistics like us have different advantages that can contribute greatly to our workplace.

We have advantages, not limitations!

# 10

# How Autistic People and Employers Develop Good Relationships

When I was young all I wanted to do was grow up! For most of my teenage years, I longed to turn eighteen so that I wouldn't have to go to school anymore. I think this is a sentiment shared by almost every teenager, not just autistic teens. I seemed to form relationships with adults much better, as I wasn't always comfortable mixing with children my own age. I always feared ridicule and exclusion; I thought that grown-ups were much more understanding and accepting of my differences and me. Back in my primary school days, I often opted to remain at a teacher's side. I found one-on-one interaction with them much easier than trying to find my place within the mob of other children. I was always naturally curious, and that curiosity encouraged me to speak to those with more wisdom—and yes, that is my ever-so-polite way of describing those older than me.

I had the belief that when I was an adult, I would be around adults who wouldn't sneer at me or question my different way of doing things. I am independent to a fault and thought that when I left school and entered the workplace, life would be so much easier for me because everyone else would be an understanding grown-up, too! As you can imagine, that hasn't always been the case. When I graduated and started working as a social worker, it was clear that I didn't work in the same way that my colleagues did. Social workers often handle large and unmanageable workloads, and it is sometimes difficult for us to prioritize. In my case, I would determine my tasks for the day and stick to them until it was time to go home. But that didn't always work the way I expected, either.

Given the nature of working with vulnerable adults and children, urgent situations arise that often cause the schedule to collapse in an instant. At that time, I wasn't good at accepting and embracing the unknown. I feared change and put additional stress on myself trying to meticulously prepare for absolutely everything. When I started in my profession, I found it difficult to cope with any form of disruption to my self-set schedule for the day. Even dealing with urgent situations, I found it hard to hide my disappointment when my schedule was ruined and that discontent could, and sometimes did, impact the rest of my working week. That caused me internal friction that was picked up by clients and my supervisors. My reluctance to acknowledge myself and accept that change happens in daily life held me back most in my working life. Fortunately, I was privileged to have very understanding colleagues who stood by me throughout my days as a practicing social worker.

Not many autistic people go through their working lives without encountering some difficulties. The world isn't really made for autistic people, which is why we often believe we must hide who we are in public or withdraw from public life completely. Once we leave school and university, it's time to make a living and try to provide for our families. In 2016, a survey carried out by the National Autistic Society highlighted that only 16 percent of autistic people are employed in the United Kingdom, but 77 percent of us want to find a job. That figure has been static since 2007.[8] It is clear that disproportionate percentages of autistic people are unemployed.

As curious as I am, I wanted to find out why this was happening. Why is it that autistic people cannot get work easily? I often marvel at the high concentration of successful autistic people throughout the ages and especially in the modern era, which pushed me to wonder why more of us aren't gainfully employed. I decided to speak directly to the autistic community to find out *why* the numbers are so low. Since I had completed a vocational university degree, finding a job as a social worker wasn't terribly difficult. I reached out to some in the community to find out what type of experiences they'd had. I received numerous responses. Kerry Chin sent me "An Employment Success Story," which demonstrates the vast possibilities that exist and how sensory issues can be readily overcome.

---

## AN EMPLOYMENT SUCCESS STORY
### *by* **Kerry Chin**

### Introduction

At the time of writing, I'm thirty-one years old. I have never been unemployed. I went from high school straight into full-time university study, and then straight into full-time work afterwards. I still work at the same company. This is unlikely enough for my generation in general, and practically a miracle for an autistic, transgender person of color like myself.

I work as an electrical engineer in the rail industry. In my career thus far, my managers have particularly appreciated my computer skills. In my current role, I spend a lot of time looking at the calendar. How's that for autism stereotypes?

## Out of University and into the Workforce

When I went to university to study electrical engineering, I thought I would eventually be working in an electricity company. I ended up in the rail industry because that was the job I got.

In my final year at university, I did not have a clear understanding of how competitive the job market was. As such, I only made a few applications to the more "obvious" employers offering graduate roles for electrical engineers. I think I only knew to try the rail company because they were at my university's career fair.

None of my other job applications progressed past the first stage. I think the main difference with the rail company was that its application form had more questions where I could distinguish myself with information beyond what was already in my resume.

The next stage of the process was an online assessment, which included numerical and verbal reasoning tests. I have always been good at these tests since the first one I did in the assessment that led to my autism diagnosis at age seven.

There was then the interview, which had individual and group components. I remember that two of the interview questions involved explaining science and engineering concepts in simple terms. I think those questions suited me, too.

As I do not have access to the internal details of the hiring process, I am only speculating about what it was that I did "right." The point is this: I got the job at the rail company. It was a two-year graduate program, in which I worked at a few different departments to gain experience in various aspects of railway electrical engineering.

**My Early Struggles**

When I first started working, I thought that I would have to spend my entire career trying to pretend I wasn't autistic. I quickly learned that pretending really wasn't an option.

Early on, the most obvious social issue I had at work was that I often did not pay attention to my own facial expression and my colleagues would then comment that I looked like I really didn't want to be there, even though that was not true. This type of comment bothered me, and my discomfort was made worse because my colleagues didn't believe my explanation that I wasn't aware of my own facial expressions.

Still, the social awkwardness was trivial compared to my sensory issues. I have sensitive hearing, and that particularly set me apart in the construction department, as most construction workers experience hearing damage caused by work site noise. One colleague even correctly guessed that I was autistic based on my ability to notice certain sounds.

At the time, the company held internal conferences for each engineering discipline, with technical presentations and networking opportunities. The catering was good at these events, but lunchtime was a nightmare for me because of the noise of everyone talking. At the time, I wasn't sure if it was socially acceptable to wear earplugs at the conference, so I didn't. I developed a headache and had to leave early. The next thing I remembered was waking up at home the next morning. That was the last time I hesitated to wear earplugs anywhere. (My supervisor subsequently ordered me a new pair of earmuffs for the next conference.)

The conferences were just two days a year. Worse still, most of the offices had fluorescent lights, which made me dizzy. At one office, I became so unwell that I thought I wouldn't make it through the year. (This was seven years ago. I survived.) I was allowed to have the light directly above my desk removed, but after that, it still took me over a year to completely recover. Along the way, I discovered the right shade of sunglasses for indoor wear.

Due to these issues, I eventually needed to disclose my autism to my managers. Reactions varied, but a particularly memorable response ("So you mean you're an engineer?") came from one of my supervisors, also an engineer himself. In context, I mentioned communication difficulties as part of being autistic, and he assumed I was just describing a stereotype of engineers. It was particularly ironic because autism-related sensory issues were a major problem for me as an engineer. (I had not antic-ipated these issues at all. I wish someone had explained my sensory issues to me earlier, but I'm also glad I didn't have this information to discourage me from pursuing this career.)

While this was not the only inappropriate comment, I have not noticed anyone treating me worse after I mentioned being autistic. More important, at every office where I have worked, I received the adjustment I requested: the removal of the light above my desk.

**From Graduate to Professional**

Despite all these challenges, I loved my job. My supervisors appreciated my work, and the pay and conditions were fairly good. Due to a company restructure at the time, my contract was extended and I ended up spending three and a half years on what was meant to be a two-year graduate program. But eventually I had to apply for a permanent role, and I found that incredibly daunting.

On the surface level, my resume looked reasonably good at the time, as I had worked in all the relevant departments for well-rounded development as an electrical engineer, but I still had difficulty writing about this experience in a way that sounded impressive.

I was lucky that the department where I was working at the time eventually advertised a position, and my day-to-day work there prepared me well to apply for it. Better still, as a graduate in that department, I had the opportunity to talk to the hiring manager. On the day before my interview, the work that I was doing prompted me to ask the hiring manager about the relationship between his team and another team. To my surprise, he explained in detail what his team did. I wrote down as much as I could, and in the interview on the following day, I realized that he had basically given me the answers to the interview questions. This was how I got my permanent role.

## Another Day, Another New Challenge

The permanent role basically involved taking bookings for equipment maintenance. (This requires technical knowledge about electrical networks. Accepting the wrong bookings can cause major disruption to train operations.)

Sometimes, the job required me to call the people who submit bookings. This helped me overcome my fear of making phone calls, because these people were generally happy to hear from me and I built up my confidence from the positive association.

I also really enjoyed the responsibility and the pressure in this role. It has taught me to become much calmer overall, which was just what I needed as I used to be a fairly nervous person. I also slept better at night than I ever did before.

Just in this role, I have had a few different managers due to turnover at that level, and learning to work with each manager was a different challenge.

In particular, one of my managers disapproved of my annual leave preferences. I often requested to take a day off every other week or so, and my manager insisted that it was a problem because it would look like I was "always on leave." This particularly bothered me because, logically, what I did actually had less impact on the company than if I took the same number of days off continuously, and yet he would prefer that.

My managers also didn't like seeing me with downtime, but as it was possible for me to clear my workload and actually have nothing to do until more work came in, this felt like I was being punished for working too efficiently.

Still, despite these issues, all of my managers agreed that I was good at what I did. In particular, they appreciated my unrivalled ability to remember what seemed like "everything" to them, including the entire calendar's worth of bookings and specific things that happened years ago.

Due to a restructure, my job title has changed and I have more responsibilities, but I have essentially been in this same job for just over five years now. This year, due to the COVID-19 pandemic, I now mostly work from home. This eliminates my issues with the office environment, and my productivity has increased. I'm happy where I am.

I consistently hear that one of the main reasons autistic people find employment opportunities so difficult to secure is the interview process, which is dreaded by most everyone. The interview format, as it stands, is very generalized. It's a one-size-fits-all format. If we don't make direct eye contact or if we are a little fidgety in our seat, we may be seen as someone who doesn't fit into that one size. That appears to be the case all over the world. If the autistic community were more aware of what a particular company's policy was on interviews, we could educate ourselves and approach the interview in a different way. We might even have a great inclination to tell our potential employer that we were autistic. It would be incredible if the interview format could provide an alternative arrangement for autistic people and others who have issues that preclude them from giving a solid interview. My experience has been that an interview is a sales pitch for oneself rather than a display of competency and expertise. I think it really shouldn't be a popularity contest where a contestant responds with the appropriate buzzwords and a forced, big, broad smile. (Although smiles are always good.) If I owned a company I would be much more focused and interested in the competency and expertise of the individual and how those traits could contribute to the overall success of my organization.

It is incredibly easy for autistic people to just give up trying because the interview method doesn't work for us. I was okay because I was able to regurgitate buzzwords, but I still found myself being ruled out of some promotions because I couldn't sell myself as a leader or torchbearer for others. Human resource officers need to realize that brilliance doesn't always include the ability to respond with an appropriate smile or comment that they feel is satisfactory. As the world moves forward, we should not be held back. I can see a future where interviews for jobs are in a different, more individualized format that gives more people a valid opportunity to express themselves. That would mean that autistic candidates might have more opportunities in the future.

## Why You Should Hire Autistic People

It is such a blessing to have a different neurotype that allows me to have an attention to detail that surpasses that of the general population. I always found it relatively easy to focus my time and schedule on what I needed to get done on a particular day. My only issue was when a sudden meeting was called or an emergency came in that I had to deal with that made my schedule for the day obsolete. Despite that, I have always been good at applying logic to emotional situations. During the times I have had to support people through a crisis, I found myself breaking the situation down into smaller and more manageable steps before determining the best way forward. My method of approaching a problem has achieved very good outcomes for the people I work with and has given me a huge sense of job satisfaction at the same time, despite the hectic nature of working as a social worker.

There is a huge misconception that autistic people are only suited to certain careers, specifically mathematical and scientific careers. In my physical and online travels, I have met many autistic people who are nurses, occupational therapists, speech therapists, and even doctors who practice in specialized fields! I agree that our minds and unique way of thinking are often suited to problem solving, but problem solving can also mean helping people work through their struggles in life, not just mathematical riddles. The very nature of our differences can help us thrive in every sector of the workforce just like anyone else, but our employment numbers don't reflect that.

According to an article by Lina Zeldovich in Spectrum, every year in the United States, one hundred thousand autistic children turn eighteen, but just 58 percent of them will gain paid employment before the age of twenty-five.[9]

There are multitudes of employment initiatives designed for autistic people worldwide that have been set up by a plethora of nonprofit groups, but the unemployment statistics for autistic people never seem to shift. Year after year there is no real increase or decrease. Some corporations have created an infrastructure and support networks for autistic people in their workplaces, not enough to have a major impact. The community believes that unemployment rates among autistic people would decrease if business owners were more aware of the abilities and capabilities of autistic workers. And I believe that if all workplaces and schools adopted a neurodiversity approach, employment rates for autistic people would skyrocket.

There is a clear economic benefit in having more autistic and neurodiverse individuals in the workforce. If businesses incorporated more autistic workers, there would be fewer of us surviving on charity or welfare. We would be contributing to those businesses' success and the economy, as well as elevating the understanding of our capabilities and talents.

Autistic people have a certain set of skills that make us the wonderful diversity group that we are. We are dependable, reliable, passionate, driven, empathetic, and determined. These things are all true; these are our gifts. There are some schools of thought that want you to believe that autistic people are reliant on routine and that, somehow, that is a negative thing. Rest assured, we will rarely be late for work; for us, and our employers, that is not a negative. It is all about having a positive outlook and approach to your career and to life in general.

An example of that positive approach to life, no matter what goals you set for yourself, is in the story of Olivia Deangelis:

## THE MERMAID
### by **Olivia Deangelis**

My name is Olivia; I am twenty-nine years old. When I was little the doctors told my parents I had mild retardation. At sixteen months old I had glasses. When I was younger my parents realized that I was smart, so they got me tested. The test results came back and said I had Asperger's. After we found out what I had, my mom sent me to the best schools to help me. She never held me back if I wanted to go on trips or to camps; she let me do it. School was the hardest for me because I was bullied really bad for being different. My mom tried her hardest to get it stopped but it didn't work. I finally stood up for myself and it worked.

As I got older and graduated from high school, my anxiety and depression got really bad because now I'm in the real world and have to look for a job for the longest time. So when I couldn't get a job, I went into some programs for people with disabilities. They were great programs but the problem was when I graduated from the programs I was back at home doing nothing, until I met these wonderful people that have a dog.

I asked them if I could walk their dog and they said yes and we became family. I still want to find a job that will be good and where I can make good money because I am on social security disability and it's not enough to live off of. My sister works, so when she's at work, I help my mom watch my sister's kids. I really love doing that. It gives me purpose.

I love everything mermaids. Last year I had a friend, her name is Michelle, who did a mermaid swim class and when

I did it, I knew I wanted to be a mermaid instructor. So she helped me get certified. I haven't taught classes but that's okay because I'm showing people if you have a dream, go for it. I also want to get married one day but I don't know if it will ever happen. My dream is to change the world for people with invisible disabilities. If it wasn't for my parents and my family I don't know where I would be.

---

I have read about programs that are designed to help autistic people and employers come together for the benefit of both. I was curious about how employers and employees create a positive relationship and reached out to autistic people to gain their perspectives on their experiences. I asked people if they would tell me their story and how their work experience could help shape future practices when it comes to employing autistic people. Christa Holmans has had experience in various jobs and they, like Olivia, appreciates the knowledge they gained early in life and a strong work ethic instilled by their mother, as well as the training classes they had the opportunity to attend.

---

## LEAVING THE NEST AND LEARNING TO FLY
### by Christa Holmans

I didn't know I was autistic when I entered the workforce at age twelve, helping my mother out in the family business. Both my mother and my father were barber-stylists. My mom raised me on her own. She's been doing hair longer than I've been alive.

Looking back on the past twenty-plus years I've been in the workforce, a massive part of my own success has been my ability to seek out and find mentors at every job.

Some people go into a new job looking for friends. When I start a new job, I look for a person who is good at their job and is willing to share and teach their knowledge to others. A good mentor is worth their weight in gold . . . maybe more!

My mom was a great workplace mentor. She's always had a strong work ethic and has been self-employed for longer than I've been alive. One of the best things my mother did for me was instilling that work ethic in me and teaching me how to be a good employee. Mom explained to me that when I'm on the clock, I need to stay busy and find things to do, otherwise I would be stealing from the company I work for. If I didn't know what else needed to be done, Mom made sure that I learned to ask my manager if I could help with anything. I learned inventory control, customer service, and even the basics behind running a business, including bookkeeping. By the time I was ready to apply for my first job outside of the family business, at the age of sixteen, I had already accumulated a nice set of workplace skills and was ahead of the game for most high school (and some college) students. The one thing I didn't know just yet was how to get through a job interview.

My next job would be in fast food, a roller-skating carhop at a popular drive-in restaurant chain. I was not required to interview for the role because I had friends on staff that vouched for me. About a year into my role as a carhop, when I was seventeen, I found myself training for an assistant manager position and started taking business and leadership courses at the chain's corporate training center. When I was a young adult, managing fast food was what I wanted to do more than anything else. I thought I would work there forever and I attended every course possible, soaking up all the training my employer was willing to give me. I found benefit in all of the full- and half-day trainings, but the training that helped me the most was the training that explained proper hiring procedures and dove deeply into the nuances behind interviewing candidates.

The peek behind that curtain let me see what hiring teams are really looking for when they ask their indirect and sometimes tricky questions. Understanding the interviewer's motives and intentions helped me reverse-engineer the interview process so that I knew to do and say the right things. It's easy to ace a test when you've memorized the answers. I've gotten myself into some great jobs in the past, even some that I wasn't qualified for, thanks to my interviewing skills.

In these classes, I learned the rules: the unwritten rules of work, what managers wanted but wouldn't say outright. I had the model for becoming the "perfect employee." Challenge accepted.

Once I learned the rules, I became a real stickler for them, and this didn't always go over well with the general manager above me, who was continually bending the rules to avoid getting into trouble with the area supervisor. Eventually, the lack of order and chaos drove me out. Just like that, the spark was gone. The spell had been broken. I was no longer in love with fast food. Mostly I was out of love with being treated like I was disposable. I had given my heart and soul.

After the drive-in, I found my way into the materials management library of one of the world's largest computer manufacturers. I was one of the first people to hold a one-terabyte hard drive when most of the world could barely imagine such a thing existed. Sworn to secrecy, I held the future in my hands.

I utilized a computer system to help a team maintain a hardware library full of top-secret technology for engineers to test. Every item had an owner and only specific users could check out certain items. If someone wanted an item that wasn't allocated to them, I would work with the hardware owner to get or deny clearance to the items.

This was one of my favorite jobs of all time. There weren't many women or people like me (gender diverse) in the organization back then, but I was at home with all the nerdy guys and engineers at the computer company. They were straightforward and practical.

I stood out in a company dominated by cis-males (a male assigned male at birth), but it almost seemed to work to my advantage. People remembered me; it made it easier for me to connect with my peers. I didn't even have to reach out; people were coming to me.

The environment was sensory-friendly, perfect for an undiagnosed autistic person who was completely unaware of their sensory needs. It was a mostly silent room, naturally lit, with the lights above my desk not too bright. We were all allowed to listen to music on headphones during the day while we worked. The environment was calm, and things were orderly because everyone meticulously followed the rules. At the end of the day, I arrived home feeling calm and relaxed. It was almost perfect until it ended very suddenly in 2008 when the economy crashed. Leaving the computer company was painful because I didn't feel done with the job and company I loved.

After the computer company, I moved through a few other jobs that weren't nearly as meaningful. By the time I was twenty-five, I'd had jobs waiting tables, worked for the state of Texas as a contractor, and spent some time in retail as a store manager. I had enjoyed jobs that let me move around and were very physical but noticed signs of wear on my body from doing physical tasks. Concerned I wouldn't be able to continue down this path for much longer, I started to look for my first office job.

At twenty-six, I landed what I thought was my dream job, working in a hip and trendy office. At the time, my autism was still unknown to me. I wouldn't know I was autistic until three years later, a few months before my thirtieth birthday.

Unfortunately, some employers expect the employee to overcome any weaknesses they have or be working towards eliminating them. This may not be possible or healthy for someone with a disability or learning difference. For example, I'll never be good at proofreading, despite lots of effort on my part to improve. A simple accommodation could have been to provide a second set of eyes or proofreading software for documents. Instead, my employer pointed out every typo I made and brought them up in my performance reviews. "Still makes the occasional typo" was typed in red on one of the documents. Years and jobs later, I still have extreme anxiety around every single email I send out, reading each one five to ten times before hitting send and sometimes retracting them a few times to double-check for typos.

It's hard when you struggle to do things that others find easy when you don't know why you struggle. You want so badly to get it right, but people around you say you're not trying hard enough. You can start to second-guess yourself.

When you've given your all and have been doing your very best, they tell you that you just need to try a little bit harder. So, you push and you push until you fail or burn out. It's soul crushing. This type of pushing eventually led me to my first significant burnout of adulthood, and ultimately, my autism discovery. Working for a company that needed me to do things their way wasn't going to cut it anymore. I needed an employer with more flexibility; my health depended on it.

My next job was with a company that specialized in HR and business consulting. This time I disclosed that I was autistic early in the interview process and was up-front with the accommodations I would need to be an all-star employee. Although legally you should not have to mention details of your disability during the early stages of the interview, I do so because an interview should be a two-way street. I need accommodations in the workplace to be successful and must see how an employer will react when I mention being autistic and my needs.

When I let the consulting firm know I would need to work remotely, instead of telling me that wasn't how they did things, I was met with curiosity and asked how working remotely would work. Eventually, the entire team was remote, and we closed the physical office.

I started off as a part-time contractor, working remotely to oversee the construction of a new website, then was brought on full-time as the marketing manager two and a half months later, before being promoted to vice president of marketing ten months after that. I worked happily with the firm for two years and eight months.

At the end of 2019, I worked within the organization to design and deliver corporate training on autistic inclusion and workplace neurodiversity. In the spring of 2020, before COVID hit the US, I was gearing up to fly around the country, speaking about my experiences as an openly autistic business professional. In March of 2020, everything changed.

Learning and development teams were hit hard and we had to adjust our service lines to compensate for the rapid changes in the economy. Eventually, layoffs became necessary, and my number was called. We cried together on the termination call that was done over Zoom. I have no hard feelings towards the firm. In fact, I'm still working with them on a few projects as an independent contractor.

For the first time in my life, being let go didn't send me into a panic. I expected to feel fear, but instead, I felt free. It felt "right." In fact, I recently thanked my old boss for "ripping the bandage off" and "pushing me out of the nest." I never would have left the team. I was loyal to them, and the uncertainty of not having a fixed income usually scares me.

There is a freedom and ease in working for yourself, knowing that you have the final say over every project and meeting that you take on, managing your own schedule, and accommodating your own needs as you see fit. Yes, it's scary knowing you're the only one responsible for "keeping the lights on" and having no guaranteed income from week to week, but at this point, I've gained way more than I've lost.

---

As Christa progressed up the business ladder, they were able to communicate their needs to their employers, who were willing to listen and make minor adjustments like removing an overhead light or exploring the option of working remotely. Looking at both sides of the same coin,

I imagine their employers probably learned a lot from them too. One of the keys for a complementary relationship between employer and employee is communication. It is an absolute necessity. Their experience is an example of what can happen when autistic people use their voices. Christa has gone from years of being successfully employed to being successfully self-employed.

There are employers around the world who want to offer opportunities to the neurodiverse community. That is a welcome and positive thought, but a basic problem remains. The training that has been and is provided to employers is ultimately holding the autistic community back. It is not as if employers are deterring us on purpose, it's just that they don't know any better. Under most current autistic employment manuals, the employer is left with a very limited perspective of what we are capable of. Based on stories I have heard, I'm certain that if employers and companies participated in neurodiversity acceptance training, the number of autistic people in the workplace would dramatically increase and both parties would be happier.

Christa's story is one that inspired me to form my company, Neurodiversity Training International (NTI). Instead of calling on others to act and do something about this, I decided to do something myself. I started a movement that informs and teaches a more accepting method and model for future generations.

Even before I started NTI, I was pleased to see things beginning to move in a direction that benefits everyone. The US government has been proactively implementing services and support for autistic people who want to enter the workforce. In 2014, the US Congress passed the Workforce Innovation and Opportunity Act. This was an incredibly bold and constructive move that required states to spend 15 percent of their budget for job-training programs on those of us who are different. Australia has also been proactive in researching the topic of unemployment within the autistic community. The thing that will keep autistic people in the workforce is the acceptance model of training so that employers don't deter, marginalize, and patronize gifted autistic people.

## Why Neurodiversity Is Needed in the Workforce

Autistic people are among the most gifted people who have ever lived! I cannot say that enough. There is so much potential and passion among us; it is a sad notion to think that a person who may have the potential to theorize a cure for a now-incurable disease is wasting away on welfare support because employers don't have the knowledge base to assimilate autistic people into their business. Employers often think they have an "autism-friendly" workplace simply because they completed training that highlights the negative things about us. I've heard from employers who suggested that they had learned that if they hired an autistic person they could experience disruptions and outbursts from individuals who did not have the capabilities to always be effective on the job. I can't say that won't happen, but I can say that disruptions at work aren't only caused by autistic people.

Demonstrated by the stories above, autistic people have diverse talents, just like absolutely everyone else. Unfortunately, traditional autism training leads employers to believe that every autistic person is the same and that everything written for the training program will apply to every autistic person who comes to work for them. That is not a factual assumption, but the statistics for the employment rates for autistic people have not increased much in the past decade, which indicates that the assumption is accepted as reality.

With all of that said, I am not naïve, either. Most everybody on the autism spectrum has difficulty with social interaction, engagement, and communication. We have other individual limitations, too, just like every other human. As proud as I am to be autistic, I don't ignore these things or live in shame of them anymore. I never dismiss that autistic people, myself included, can and do struggle with certain aspects of life. Working with businesses and corporations while teaching ourselves to discover our voice, recognize our talents, and utilize them, we can create a dynamic experience for everyone involved.

There are many good reasons why autistic people have the potential to thrive in the workplace. Some of these might include excellent memory, often above-average intelligence, proficiency in problem solving, and—most of all—reliability. Obviously not every autistic person will meet these criteria. But, if an employer will have a thoughtful discussion with the autistic employee, they can generally reach a conclusion about how they can support each other. The best way for an employer to do that would be to ask the potential employee what they think they are good at and where they feel they might perform best in the organization. That is a positive approach that will allow the autistic person to talk about what their passions are and how they might contribute. It also provides the employer an opportunity to understand the extent of their future employee's abilities. It requires honest communication and an open mind from both parties: inclusive unity.

As a training provider myself, I like to look at the training others provide to create opportunities for autistic people. I signed up for an online session, and to say it disheartened me would be the biggest understatement of my life. The training was full of exclusion instead of inclusion, such as ushering an autistic employee somewhere quiet when they are distressed, excluding autistic employees from important tasks such as counting money, and keeping them away from the general public due to the risk of people finding them rude. I was anonymous during the training course. I didn't introduce myself as autistic and I joined the discussion via the chat box in the webinar. I felt like an autistic James Bond. I stated very clearly that in none of the training slides did it mention having discussions with the autistic employees themselves. The trainer retorted that autistic people often have difficulty expressing themselves and that colleagues may have to act. I demonstrated that autistic people can express themselves and it got me ejected from the webinar.

The one thing that the autistic community has is something that money can't buy: it's the fact we are autistic and know what it is like. Most training and development is written and delivered by people who do not know what it is like to be different and rely solely on their own interpretations and perceptions.

Throughout this chapter, I hope that I have demonstrated that autistic people can thrive in the workplace, if only the right attitude is applied. No amount of training and development will help you get to know an autistic employee better than sitting down and letting them tell you about themselves.

I always knew what I was good at, what areas I needed improvement in, and the tasks I wasn't very good at. When I admitted them and started telling people about them, my working life became much easier. One skill that I see many of my colleagues use is the art of being able to talk on the phone while receiving instructions from someone else in the room. When I am on the phone, the outside world could be descending into a zombie apocalypse and I won't know until my phone call is finished. If I am on the phone and someone whispers, "Come and see me when you are done with that call," I will not absorb this command and the person making the request will be waiting an awfully long time for me to delight them with my presence. I don't multitask while on the phone.

In a few of the offices that I have worked in, I always created a reason to go in and meet with the boss before I started the job. This allowed me to become familiar with my working space and ease the nerves that I knew would accompany my first actual day of work. It certainly helped me and it is something I recommend that all employers offer to new autistic employees. In fact, it may actually help all employees, autistic or not. When I have spoken with others, they admitted that they had done something similar and it seemed to be helpful for them too.

For those of us who are sensitive to sound, it gives us an idea of how noisy the workplace environment is or how much space there is and, in general, a greater idea of what to expect. It's similar to the ritual I use before I speak before groups of people. It helps me effectively acclimatize myself to a new environment.

In the United Kingdom, the Equality Act is a huge saving grace for everyone, regardless of ability. In this piece of legislation, it is illegal for employers to discriminate against people who are different, no matter what the difference is. That is a good thing. The act doesn't just cover the day-to-day duties of the job itself but also covers interview arrangements, terms and conditions, redundancy, and even dismissal. The act also legislates for "reasonable adjustments" to be made to accommodate everyone. In my own case, I was provided with an office with fewer people in it, and that helped me. However, these accommodations and adjustments are only possible through thoughtful discussions between autistic people and employers. As I learned quite abruptly, even though joining the workforce is an achievement, the red carpet isn't automatically rolled out for us, and most people are not mind readers. Autistic people have to take responsibility and communicate to ensure that the work environment gives them the best chance of success.

Autistic people can bring so much value to any workplace. With our drive, passion, and reliability, we can possess skills high above average but still find ourselves unemployed, more so than others. The more employers know about neurodiversity and acceptance, the better!

Many people think that they are being helpful to autistic employees and colleagues by making concessions, but in reality, it is quite patronizing and actively deters autistic people from finding employment for themselves. I know that if my bosses kept me away from everyone else or avoided giving me certain responsibilities because they thought I couldn't handle it, I wouldn't be very keen to work, either! I don't believe that many would disagree with me on that point.

It is very difficult to capture the diversity of our community in a few presentation slides or lectures, but one thing that can be captured is negativity. And it spreads like wildfire. Governments can spend whatever they want on making every workplace in the world "autism friendly" but if the programs don't impart real facts, they are not being friendly. Governments and employers alike need to become "neurodiversity aware" and "difference friendly" and provide a more individualized approach, because what could change those outmoded concepts are "neurodiversity-friendly" workplaces, designed in conjunction with neurodiverse individuals!

# 11

# Why Are Autistic Lives So Short?

This is a difficult chapter to write, and it will be difficult to read for some. It is, however, an important reality that the autistic community lives with. It's something that affects every single person in our lives, as it does us. Although studies are being conducted, there are no definitive reasons behind our shortened life spans. It is a reality that doesn't have many answers or any rationale, yet it exists. The fact is, statistically, people with autism live shortened lives.

On the 7th of August 2020, I turned thirty years old. It was a celebration, and I had a lovely time! It was a hollow day, though, because I was now thirty; it was coming close to the time when people like me die. I couldn't help but be drawn to research articles from multiple online sources that stated that the average life span of an autistic person is between thirty-six and fifty-four years old, depending on the publication.[10]

A verified article in *Psychology Today* states that a study published in April 2017 in the *American Journal of Public Health* found "the life expectancy in the United States of those with ASD to be thirty-six years old as compared to seventy-two years old for the general population."[11]

When I first heard this, I was incredibly shocked. I read and researched as extensively as I could, and the results were clear: we die sooner than the general population. One study carried out in Sweden monitored the health of autistic people for a twenty-year time frame.[12] Many people never made it through the research because they died during the study. This information, and more, is available online, and it makes for very sobering reading.

Those who are autistic with accompanying learning disabilities seemed to pass closer to the age of thirty-six. There were several reasons—including epilepsy, choking episodes, and domestic accidents—that accounted for some participants passing prior to the end of the research term. Autistic people living in institutional care also accounted for some higher death rates.

It is a scary thought; the closer I am to thirty-six, the more my chances of an early demise increase. That is a life-altering reality that has made me pay close attention to what life actually means to me. Since I became aware of this, I have enjoyed the simple things in life much more. I give Ethan an extra hug when he wants one, I call my mother daily, and I try to enjoy as many social occasions as I can, crowds permitting. Of course, no research studies can determine the outcome of everyone. I could still grow old into my eighties or nineties even though my chances of living to and through my golden years are greatly reduced. It is heartbreaking to realize that many parents, siblings, friends, and associates of autistic people may have to say goodbye sooner than they want.

I wouldn't describe myself as the most animated person ever to have lived. A lot of the time I am quite blank and come across as someone who doesn't get excited very easily. That is just who I am. I often say that my "receiving a book deal" face and my "having only a few weeks to live" face are very much the same and indistinguishable by the naked eye. When I am passionate about a topic, I can—and often do—become much more animated, like when I am speaking to promote the rights of autistic people and to highlight that we often leave this world too early.

## My Own View on Mental Health

Living in a dungeon that is completely constructed by the mind is a terrifying experience. Most young children play games, get up to mischief, and love the world around them. I didn't. To the five-year-old Jude Morrow, the world was a loud and chaotic place that seemed similar to a constant apocalypse. My school playground was a hornet's nest of noise that lacked direction. I stood in the confines of my dungeon and refused to play any part of what was happening on the outside of that mental boundary. I felt anxious and shy because I knew I wasn't like the other kids. And, yes, the fear of rejection does exist, even in the youngest of children. You can take my word on that.

I was always told that I was "awkward," "anti-social," and "a loner." I felt like I was imprisoned and confined to the dungeon that other children, teachers, and society had built around me.

Like a good little boy, I stayed within the confinement of their prison and looked out at the other children laughing and playing. Like the detainees of the Tower of London, I was in solitary confinement looking out as the world continued on with life. In my solitude, I began to read and write. My parents were there with me. They encouraged and loved me no matter what. They always told me how great I was and that one day I would prosper. I never believed it. I felt I was locked in the dungeon and wasn't really allowed to leave. I attempted to escape at times, but outside rejections made me stay up there; I decided to use the time to perfect my craft of reading and writing, and I loved it. Even though I nurtured my passion and talent, I was basically institutionalized in a judgment dungeon.

By all accounts, I was quite successful as an adult. I was a father, a social worker, an author, and a lecturer, and yet the tower of imprisonment still loomed over me. But there came a time when this tower that had been constructed around me started to impact my relationship with my infant son. I fell back into the belief that I wasn't good enough, that I had too many deficiencies, and that I would never integrate into society successfully, even though I was an employed, home-owning parent! Those and other details meant that I was integrated, at least in my understanding. I came to a point in my life where I realized that I had to learn to love and accept myself as an autistic man.

The thought that I could love myself never occurred to me, as my experience had been that if I were open about this fact, I would be judged. But I knew I needed help. I received that in the form of psychotherapy and cognitive behavioral therapy (CBT). I worked hard to better myself, loose the angst, and become comfortable with who I am. In that process I realized that the tower represented societal misconceptions about autism. I believed that people and their judgments had locked me away. Was this factual? I decided to take a brave step. Standing inside the imprisonment tower, I tried the door handle and realized that the door was open!

I walked down the stairs and took an instant hit of fresh air. What I hadn't realized was that the door had always been open and a large part of the tower's construction was designed and built by me! With that knowledge, I could walk around freely, go wherever I wanted, and watch as the tower crumbled.

I reflected on my time in the tower and remembered nurturing my love of reading and writing, which I turned into my debut book, *Why Does Daddy Always Look So Sad?* As a self-accepting adult, I started to view my childhood in a different way. Not that I was subjected to constant defeat but that I had so many victories that I had lost count of them.

I have a fondness for this tower, though. When I speak to audiences, I always speak about the time I spent there and how I eventually had to take responsibility . . . and a giant leap of faith. Many autistic people feel imprisoned in their own minds. The lesson I share with everyone is that if you feel trapped in a tower with a similar architecture to mine, always try the door handle.

In truth, I was my own worst enemy, as many of us are. I knew I needed support, knowledge, and guidance pertaining to my mental health, but for vast sections of my teenage years and early adulthood, I didn't take advantage of the assistance. It was quite easy to assume the role of the victim and feel that nobody supported or understood me. I knew that I needed help raising my mood, yet I constantly refused any aid out of defiance and pride. Frankly, everyone needs to take responsibility for their own mind and realize that it is okay to discuss what is troubling you. I did it and it truly helped me.

People can, and do, become disillusioned with public services or healthcare services, especially when it comes to mental health. I certainly felt that way, and it took me quite some time to find people I was comfortable with, who really understood me and didn't try to fix who I am. It would have been quite easy to give up and blame inadequate healthcare structures when it came to addressing my mental health issues, but I persevered, and it was the best decision I ever made. I took responsibility for my own well-being; I didn't give up, and it has paid dividends ever since. I would urge everyone to do the same.

## Autistic People and Suicide

Numerous studies such as the twenty-year retrospective conducted by University of Utah Health have contributed to the awareness of suicide within the autistic community.[13] The data from a variety of sources is alarming.[14]

Much of it indicates that autistic adults are eight times more likely to take their own lives, suicide among autistic females is higher than in females who are not autistic,[15] and suicides among autistic teenagers have been increasing year over year for the past decade.

Given my own mental health struggles, I can understand why these statistics and studies highlight such stark findings. I was always particularly good at hiding what I was feeling and thinking and, sadly, many others in the autistic community are too. One of the primary reasons is because the system fundamentally doesn't allow us to be ourselves. It does the opposite; it encourages us to live a lie. The lie is that we have to mimic the vast majority of people. Unfortunately, the neurotypical population has also experienced an increase in suicide rates. I hope that they, as well as the neurodiverse population, learn from the experiences of others and seek help and ways to combat the stress of today's life.

Generally speaking, males on the spectrum commit suicide more than females.[16] However, the statistics relating to gender and autism might be misleading. They indicate that autism is more prevalent in boys when girls are often underdiagnosed. According to some of the research, the main reason autistic females take their own lives can be attributed to a lack of diagnoses and support.[17] Thankfully, more and more autistic women are speaking out about their experiences and their life on the spectrum. But the numbers are still low and the awareness needs to grow.

I have heard too many sad stories from people who tried to get help but found that what was provided wasn't adequate. I asked some of them to add their voice to these pages but, understandably, most are reluctant. They have not gone through the tunnel to the point that they are comfortable in the light. So, I will share more of my experience.

This is an issue I related to, as well. I found it very difficult to speak to professionals about how I felt. It was hard not to get defensive and completely dismiss what counselors and therapists tried to tell me. When I did find a counselor who was able to help me, she highlighted alexithymia, which is the difficulty in verbalizing emotions. This is something I have always struggled with, but over time I have improved. Through my CBT sessions I found a useful tool that I use. For me it was beneficial to write down what I felt and come back to it later to review and interpret it. I did this between sessions with my therapist and developed the ability to better express myself.

The inability to verbalize emotions is an impediment that can be reduced with professional help. But if an autistic child has undergone compliance therapies and agrees with everything a therapist says while having difficulty expressing emotions, they will not receive proper care and attention. The child is not communicating what he or she honestly feels; they are simply conforming to what they have been told is correct, which is "agree, no matter what you actually feel."

Something must change. A higher level of awareness of alexithymia would be a good start. Finding ways for people on the spectrum to recognize and examine their emotions so that they can be verbally addressed is important. Maybe it's as simple as my way of writing down and reflecting on my thoughts between sessions. Access to therapists who encourage the honest and free verbalization of emotional responses would be a tremendous help to us. It requires two people to begin communication, and that can save a life. These types of supportive aids should be the gold standard for communication with people on the spectrum. If even one life is saved, it is worth it!

## Some Little-Known Truths

There is some debate out there regarding the life expectancy of autistic people. The numbers you hear most often are thirty-six to fifty-four years. It is quite a large margin, although it is still much younger than everyone else in the general population. There is a great deal of misuse of terminology when researchers say "those who are more autistic" or "higher on the spectrum" (i.e., those with severe intellectual disabilities) die younger. In many cases that is true. Whichever way one decides to examine the research and statistics, one thing is clear: we do die much sooner than our non-autistic counterparts.

I have mentioned this fact many times when being interviewed. I have said that many of us don't live to see our retirement; it seems to be something that needs to change within our society and one of the greatest social injustices plaguing our planet. My statements have often been met with ridicule when I discuss this topic. Some go so far as to say that someone "lower on the spectrum," like me, doesn't really have to worry about such a statistic. As I stated previously, the spectrum is not a sliding scale that determines how autistic one is or isn't. It's a circle where everyone in the community holds a place. None of us are better or worse than another. We may have different abilities, or lack thereof, but that doesn't mean we aren't all autistic. People don't seem to understand that although I can converse, write books, tolerate an airport for short amounts of time, and drive, I am still an autistic man and this is an issue we face, individually and as a community.

As a child, I often decided to go where my legs would carry me, which was often the opposite direction that my parents and teachers wanted me to go. I have been a keen explorer throughout my life, and I always wondered why I had to stay with the rest of the group. Of course, like many other children, I wasn't mature enough to understand that I was putting myself at risk for accidents, of which I had many. I fell, I got lost, and thankfully I was able to find my way back again. No matter what adventure I took off on, my family was there, supporting me. My parents and older sister always "got" me and believed in me from the day I was born right up to this very day. I know they will always have my back and be my biggest fans. Unfortunately, there are some parents out there who do not have the same mind-set or belief in their children.

I understand that this may be difficult to read and absorb because it is such a departure from what most of us experience. But it should be addressed. We need to illuminate the darkness.

The chances of an autistic child being killed by a parent or caregiver are much higher than other children.[18] This is also true for children who have some form of physical or cognitive differences. There are a variety of reasons parents and caretakers give, ranging from accidents to negligence to a mental break.[19]

One of the first items I came across in the media that seemed to make this a sympathetic issue for the parents happened in the Alex Spourdalakis case. According to the *Daily Mail*, Alex was killed by his mother because she "became overwhelmed when Alex's condition deteriorated outside the hospital."[20] A documentary has been made about that murder. *Forbes* followed up with a comprehensive piece that queries, "If a Parent Murders an Autistic Child, Who Is to Blame?"[21]

There have been cases of an adult taking the life of an autistic child because the adult couldn't handle the stress they say was caused by the child.[22] A quick online search will shed light on the prevalence of these types of cases.[23] The worst part of this is that when these cases go to trial, a high level of stress is often used as the defensive strategy.[24] That claim makes it appear that the adult was justified in murdering the child or person entrusted to their care.

There's a contradiction that I see in child murder cases. If an adult murders a non-autistic child, it horrifies society. But when a child on the spectrum is murdered, sympathy often seems to be removed from the victim, the child, and deposited on the parent or caregiver who committed the crime. Excuses like, "They required constant care" or "It was too much for me to handle" or "They had to be restrained" are common. Basically, the adult is claiming that the burden of caregiving was too much for them to deal with, and sometimes these acts are even referred to as "a mercy killing."

Obviously, no one celebrates a death, yet in most of these cases, the public relates more to the murderer than to the victim. I am not dismissing the fact that parents are faced with stressors but, to me, stress or the inability to cope is not a viable excuse to kill. In today's world there are many organizations that can help parents in any number of ways, including supporting their mental health. And, in my opinion, these types of defensive strategies tarnish the memory of the poor child who has lost their life.

## Years of Masking Are Catching Up!

I, like many autistic people, masked who I was from the people around me. I was encouraged to "be myself," but how could I "be myself" when most people viewed my unique way of doing things as wrong? When I was "myself," teachers found it difficult and uncomfortable when I suddenly wanted to leave my seat and stretch my legs by walking around the classroom. When I was "myself," teachers told me to stop obsessing about or repeating songs that I liked or books that I'd read. When I was "myself," I was encouraged to join in with group activities when I preferred to work alone. So "myself" never got to be "myself."

I thought I ought to go along with people's requests and expectations to the point where I often found it difficult to say no to anybody! This is an example of how I can be largely compliant and even a people pleaser: when asked to do public engagements, I often say yes before the proposer finishes their sentence. Even as a grown man, the lingering doubt of whether I am doing the right thing or not is incredibly tiring. At social occasions I often wonder if I am standing in the right position when being photographed, giving my best effort to contribute to small talk, or responding with the correct facial expressions so that I don't come across as rude or disinterested.

As a child, I observed how other children greeted each other, continuing through my mid-teens. I read books and didn't mingle very often, so my language skills were as unique as me. My verbiage was like an eighteenth-century political diplomat compared to other children my age. Verbalizing thoughts the way other people might didn't—and still doesn't—come naturally to me. For me, it requires the same amount of effort as speaking a foreign language.

Of course, all these worries gather in the mind to form a perfect pool of anxiety. With anxiety comes the personally asked question, "Why am I always on edge?" This can lead to depressive episodes.[25] Personally, I want to state categorically that I am not anxious or depressive because I am autistic. I am anxious and depressive as I sometimes still feel that I cannot be my authentic self. I am not alone in this. People on the spectrum carry the burden of not being generally accepted; they experience the painful compliance ideas that are still prevalent. I, like many others, conditioned myself to care very deeply about what other people think of me.

Misconceptions also play a part in our mental health. I have a good memory but not on the savant level. Whenever I tell people that I am autistic, sometimes they assume that I like to sit alone at home and memorize bus and train timetables. This simply isn't true; I like to sit alone at home and look up *Titanic* stuff. There's sometimes an assumption that autistic people are mathematical and numerical geniuses; while in the savant community this may be true, it isn't true for all of us, including me. I have met numerical geniuses and they amaze me in the same way they are amazed at my knowledge of words and language.

This is an opportune moment to talk about another misconception that, like all of them, must be viewed through an individualized lens. It is the concept that autistic people cannot feel empathy. Imagine reading or hearing that you cannot feel empathy like other people can. Like every human being, I can be prone to bouts of selfishness and carelessness, but I certainly am not incapable of considering other people and what they are experiencing. We may not express our feelings in the same way as neurotypical people, but that doesn't mean we don't have emotional feelings. Empathy is a regular human emotion, one that we feel too. For the world to widely believe that autistic people are not too far removed from robots is, frankly, depressing. There are those who understand autistic people and neurodiversity very well, but if you ask someone who doesn't know a lot about autism or autistic people, they will usually use the description "lack of empathy" as a "symptom."

What appears on my face doesn't necessarily reflect what is going on in my heart. I can feel intense sadness for others and I can "walk in their shoes" quite easily. Just because I don't show it very well at times doesn't mean it's not there. Think of a game of poker. If a player has pocket aces and another has two cards off-suit that aren't a pair, both of their faces will remain the same. Does that mean neither player is excited or disappointed? No, they just have expressionless faces that hide what they are feeling. When my grandmother died, I was able to imagine what it would be like losing my own mother. I dare not even try and imagine a world where I can't share my victories, disappointments, and happiness with my mother. While I may struggle to know exactly what to do in a situation, I can certainly understand and appreciate the issues that other people have and empathize with them.

## Autism and Underlying Health Conditions

As I have stated, I generally don't approve of much of the research into the autistic community, especially the research that seeks to cure, fix, and "normalize" us. Research that I absolutely approve of is the link between autism and other physical health conditions.

### Gastrointestinal (GI) Disorders

A specific issue that seems to be highlighted quite frequently in this research is gastrointestinal (GI) problems. No one is quite sure why our community suffers from GI issues, and research continues in that arena. I fit into that category because I'm prone to occasional bouts of colitis and have had gastric problems from childhood. I had duodenal ulcers and am still prone to indigestion and heartburn. I know that my taste for fast food doesn't help this matter! Some things are just too good to give up completely.

It has been estimated that autistic children suffer from these GI issues three times as often as neurotypical children.[26] Common symptoms include vomiting, constipation, abdominal pain, acid reflux, and diarrhea. When a youngster has any of these problems—and especially when the child cannot communicate what they are experiencing—it can be extremely frustrating for both the child and the adult. Several parents have told me that they modify diets when their child has GI problems. They usually remove gluten and dairy from their child's diet and sometimes report great success. I would not be a good candidate for that diet due to my love of pizza, cold milk, and sandwiches. I haven't ever attempted to remove gluten or dairy from my diet, but it is something I would consider in future should I have severe issues.

I have also spoken with parents who found that probiotics promoted good digestive health for their kids. Probiotics are live microorganisms that many people claim improve and balance the GI system and help aid digestion. The good bacteria in probiotics are even recommended by some doctors as a method of keeping your immune system healthy. This is important for everyone, but especially those of us on the spectrum.

Then there is stress and its effect on the GI tract. People have described me as someone who feels stress much more acutely than the average person. I certainly agree with this, and I am not immune to having a hissy fit should a certain situation not go my way. A good example would be if I have my entire workday planned out and then must deal with a sudden emergency. As I have said, I do not do the unexpected well. While I always manage to keep my exterior professionalism, internally I can struggle. This does add to stress, which is a huge contributory factor in gastrointestinal health issues that include irritable bowel syndrome (IBS) and its related conditions.

## Stress

The stress of all the factors in a neurodiverse life causes not only emotional pain but physical pain too. It also affects your emotional responses, ability to think, and behaviors. It can contribute to stomach distress, headaches, chest pain, and lack of sleep. It has been cited as the leading cause of premature deaths.[27]

Is it any wonder autistic children and adults face higher levels of anxiety? Constantly having to fit in with everyone and do what is expected of us all the time is completely exhausting and driving us to our graves.

There are standard ways to help manage stress. They include accepting things that are beyond your control, exercising, eating healthy, and taking time for yourself to cultivate areas that you find relaxing like painting, writing, or dancing. These methods of releasing stress don't cure us or fix us; they help by letting us be ourselves in a healthier way.

## Epilepsy

Epilepsy is another condition that many in the autistic community face. The symptoms can vary in severity and range from fixed staring episodes to frequent grand mal seizures. The seizures are bad enough, but the falls that can occur from them can cause acute injuries. I have never been afflicted with seizures as such, but occasionally I can stare into space and not absorb what people are saying to me. I certainly can have lapses in my attention span, although I don't have epilepsy.

Research has shown that autistic people with underlying learning disabilities are more likely to have seizures.[28] Seizures and epilepsy can afflict autistic people at any point in their lives, although the vast majority experience symptoms from an early age. It is heartbreaking for epileptic children, especially the younger ones, to have to experience what they experience. There are many medical treatments and therapies that reduce the chances of having seizures and allow a great quality of life. And there are many outlets that offer advice and support to those living with epilepsy. I would encourage everyone to use them, even if it is just to speak with someone going through the same thing.

## Lack of Sleep

Many times, I find myself awake at night. My mind only goes at two speeds: the speed of light—all 186,282.397 miles per second of it—

or sleep. There doesn't seem to be much in between. When my mind and thoughts travel at the speed of causality, more widely known as the speed of light, I struggle to get the rest I need. This has always been the case for me. Some of my earliest memories are of climbing into my parents' bed in the small hours of the morning or playing in the living room watching the sunrise as my mother looked on gracefully, despite her own lack of sleep. Sometimes when I go to sleep, I awaken suddenly in the middle of the night and I just exist, fully awake, until it's time to go to work or take Ethan somewhere fun. In fact, some portions of this book and my previous book were written in the middle of the night because of my chronic sleep troubles.

A lack of sleep for any person can cause health complications that accumulate as the years go by. Lack of sleeping can increase the risk of developing heart disease, diabetes, and even strokes. Parents often ask me about my sleep patterns as a child because they are concerned about their own child or children. I didn't take any medication like melatonin when I was young, although I did take sleeping medications when I was older. In the pharmaceutical world, there isn't a magic pill or medicine for absolutely everything. There are treatments out there that assist sleep, and one of my favorites for a restful sleep was exercise. When I was running marathons and more physically active, I did sleep much better.

Everything combined depletes my energy stores. I am much too fond of an afternoon nap for a man my age, and I am more suscepti-ble to occasional bouts of sickness, stress, and generally being down. I often believe that this is what the older generation must feel like after many decades of hard craft. I never slept very well, and my façade of being like everyone else is like the ordinary person working for eigh-teen or so hours a day from the age of five!

Sleep deprivation has been shown to increase the risk of prema-ture death in all people. In the autistic community, sleep problems are much more prevalent and are a key ingredient in our lower life expectancy.

## You Are Not Alone

Given my social work background, I am all for social justice and social models of disability. That's exactly what neurodiversity is. It's a social model. There can be millions of breakthroughs in medical imaging, pharmaceutical treatment, and medication, but the best source of support, in my opinion, is to know that you aren't alone. I have worked with several service user groups in my career, and the one thing that seems to help the vast majority is the support group.

This is an outlet for people to share their experiences, gain advice from others, and even establish friendships. From a medical standpoint, support is only given periodically and for a specific purpose. That's good for some things. But from a truly productive standpoint, group support is at the top of the list. All it takes is one small piece of advice or nugget of gold from someone going through the same things you are to make your life infinitely easier. The ability to confide in someone else who personally knows what you are experiencing and has the capacity to explore measures to improve your life is truly a gift. I suggest everyone find a group and explore ways to develop yourself, share your fears and your dreams, and find ways to be who you are!

## Everyone Has a Role

Autistic people finally have the fundamental opportunity to speak up and have their voices heard. There are countless individual experiences and circumstances that are worth listening to. My story is published but there are many more out there, especially online. The difficulty is when people share their experiences and are dismissed. Imagine sharing a painful and private part of your life and someone responds, "Oh, it couldn't have been that bad." I know what it is like to be dismissed; it's painful. When I tell people about my life, I am often told that I am "not that autistic" or I am "quite low on the spectrum." What does that mean, and who are they to make such a determination?

It's a phenomenon called gaslighting. It's a psychological method of making someone question their own reality. Whenever someone's experiences, their truth, and their heartfelt honesty are summarily dismissed, it invokes a sense of guilt from the person telling their story. This must stop! We are entitled to share our experiences of life, just as everyone is. We must continue to speak up and be heard.

## Adopt a Social Model

Educational outlets should adopt a social model when it comes to autistic people. We need to have access to each other, to learn from each other. The medical model serves other serious illnesses, but for us, it doesn't really apply. As previously stated, many professionals who are in training learn the old, common, and unfavorable views of autism that are most damaging. Those perspectives of negative stereotypes keep us ostracized and excluded from the opportunities that would give us the quality of life we deserve. Many current teaching methods seek to highlight aspects of our culture that seem inhuman to the vastly neurotypical population. With that educational background and that mind-set, the professionals feel we are better served if we fall in line with them. I wonder how they would feel if we decided they should fall in line with us. Is that fair to anyone? No, it is not. We are each individuals who should be received and accepted as unique. Use research to support and understand us—not fix, cure, or change us.

## Appreciation

There is something very meaningful about being autistic. It makes me who I am, and those closest to me love me for it. The passion it brings to me flows through the pages of this book. I am not the only one who feels this way. The growing numbers of autistic voices proclaiming how being autistic is meaningful for them is both staggering and inspiring. *It is time we respect our neurodiversity so that others in the world can also respect it!*

Appreciation should not stop there. It should flow into everything around us. We are alive and have the ability to make our lives what we want. Our goals may differ but we can all appreciate the fact that we can reach for them. True, we may face obstacles. That's okay. Everyone on the planet faces their own individualized problems. We can even appreciate obstacles because they teach us what we don't want to participate in.

Beyond the traditional appreciation of family, friends, teachers, employers, and life in general, we—and our family and friends—should appreciate our community. We are the basis for our ever-expanding comfort zone. We can bounce ideas around and even disagree without a sense of being judged. Our autistic community should be beyond appreciated. It should be cherished. It gives us a basic sense of belonging; it helps us grow, understand, develop, and expand as individuals and as a community and opens the door of possibility to the neurotypical world.

## Educators and Employers

Imagine the difference if every teacher and employer in the world had a general understanding that people can be, and are, proud to be different. Imagine those differences being supported rather than criticized. The environment of school or work would change drastically. A wonderful example is a teacher I had when I was nine. I speak about him frequently because he had such a healthy impact on my life. He could see that I was a confident reader and encouraged me to get involved with our school plays. This was a role I excelled in, as I was able to project my voice and stand onstage with the rest of my classmates. I was also given the classroom responsibility for making sure our little library was tidy at the back of the classroom and I remember it giving me a feeling I hadn't felt very often up to that point: I felt that, in my own way, I fit in and I felt important and equal. I was part of the group and I had a sense of belonging. With my newfound responsibilities, I felt trusted and devoted extra care and attention to my tasks so that I would be asked to do more tasks. My parents gave me tasks to do around the house and it made me feel like an integral member of the household, not someone who held everyone else back. But having a teacher acknowledge that I was capable and trustworthy helped make me feel like I was part of the human family.

*Teachers have the chance to be heroes!* They can brighten the lives of autistic children in their classroom by making them feel needed, wanted, involved, important, and trusted. Nurturing the talents of autistic people as opposed to constantly seeking to change us will help us join the world with our own talents.

The same advice holds true for any workplaces that have autistic or neurodiverse people in them. You can make a difference that will not only benefit your autistic employee but will reflect favorably on you and your business, as you've read in the stories in previous chapters.

Don't set us up to fail by comparing us to others in search of our weaknesses. Put a greater focus on our strengths and abilities. The good feelings that surge through our bodies when we feel we are part of something, when we feel we are trusted, those are what will help autistic people live longer, happier, and more fulfilled lives.

Being thirty years old frightens me because it means I am potentially in the winter of my life. In a few short years I will be within the average age bracket that suggests I will die. All the years of people trying to support me, with their hearts in the right places, could have a detrimental effect on me and shorten my natural life. I hope I live to be elderly, I really do. I want to experience the wonder and magic of having grandchildren, an experience that my parents absolutely love. I want to experience the joy they have whenever they see Ethan or my two nephews, Jake and Adam. I have many more things that I want to accomplish and milestones to meet. The sad thing is that the odds are stacked against me, but it isn't too late for the generations of autistic children that follow me.

Like any writer, I don't want my work to age. I want it to be timeless. I hope that if someone is reading this book one hundred years after publication, they will be in shock that, at one point in human history, autistic people didn't have the same life expectancy as everyone else. It is my hope that this statistic is consigned to history, never to return.

# 12

# Where Do We Go from Here?

Throughout this book, I have tried to provide inspiration and hope through the autistic voices that have so bravely told their stories. The autistic community is a proud one and only growing prouder by the day. Thankfully, there are numerous neurodiversity advocacy groups that are helping bring power to the words "acceptance" and "understanding" rather than "diagnose" and "cure."

I am no expert. I haven't done hundreds of hours of research of my own to qualify this as a technical paper (it isn't). But I know what I am! I am an autistic person who is part of a community that is very misunderstood by others. No matter how inclusive and understanding people may think they are, there remain accepted descriptions of us that portray a disenfranchised, unfeeling, nonemotional, uncommunicative group of individuals who don't fit into society. That is not what we see in ourselves! Even though the terminology "autism awareness" has increased in use, it just means that people are more "aware" of the adverse ideas that have been used to describe us. That view of awareness lists all the "traits," "symptoms," or "negative behaviors" that many feel we have—even though we know we have more wonderful gifts to contribute to the world than unfavorable qualities.

We also know that if children grow into adulthood believing they are fundamentally flawed, they have little chance of succeeding at anything. When a child is embedded with the concept that they are incapable of achieving, they usually won't try. If an inspirationally reinforced approach is used with a child, they will mature being happier in their own skin, better adjusted, far more confident, and capable of success, and they will carry a sense of pride throughout their life. This has to come from parents and teachers and people the child looks up to, and it begins by letting the child communicate their interests. When those interests are supported and allowed to bloom, children grow with a sense of connectedness and are more likely to discover more about themselves.

My goal for this book is that it serves to open discussions and promote progressive thoughts in the autistic community, those who live with and love them, and the educators and professionals who work with them, as well as the rest of the world that could use our experiences as examples of how to and how not to treat each other. I hope it provides a general guideline as to how to tackle issues that the autistic community must live with every single day. We want the world to join with us and celebrate our individuality as we recognize the wonderfully diverse group that we are. All we ask for is what everyone deserves: respect. We are not perfect, but no one is. We just want the world to see us through our eyes.

If I were an autistic Moses, the following takeaways would be carved on my stone tablets.

## Please Use Language the Autistic Community Prefers

For those of us who want to celebrate the fact that we are autistic, state "I am autistic." Saying someone "has" autism promotes and propagates the cognitive impairments associated with "having" cancer or "having" any other horrible or incurable illness that exists in modern medicine. For most of us, being autistic is meaningful and wonderful. It makes us the incredible people we are.

And for parents who fear that their child is autistic, channel that fear into constructive support and recognition of the gifts your child brings to the world. My parents had fears for me, as is natural for most parents who have a newly diagnosed child. My parents look back on my childhood with some regret that their fear for my future often consumed them. If they were able to leap from the year 2000 to 2020, they would have enjoyed my childhood a little bit more. In any case, my parents accepted and loved me for who I was and never sought to force me to change. I was the only person who believed I was broken, and it took me a long time to discover that I wasn't and to recover from the misplaced view of myself.

It took many years to accept the fact that I am autistic. Not only have I accepted it, but I also wear it like a badge of honor on any stage I speak on, in any training session I deliver, and wherever I go in the world. The autistic community largely rejects the term "having" autism. So please, listen to us and respect our choice. We are autistic and we are proud.

The term "autism spectrum disorder," commonly called ASD, should also be revised because we do not have a disorder; we just do things in our own wonderful way. It may be a different order, but it's not a disorder. The neuromajority always seem to decide what a disorder is; hence, they label us with that term simply because we don't do things in the same way the majority does things.

I am not saying, nor have I ever said, that autistic people do not need support or guidance. At times I need support. I may require additional clarification when I am delegated certain tasks, or I may need more reassurance that I am doing things to the standards people expect of me. I am happy to benefit from any support I am given from colleagues, my family, my girlfriend, and even my son. They support me because they want me to thrive and be the best version of myself, not because they want me to change to be like them. That is the key: whenever autistic people are being supported, it should be to help them do things in their own way, not the way the majority prefer.

There seems to be an automatic cognitive association where the word "autism" is used to describe those with learning disabilities. I can't acknowledge enough that there are autistic people with intellectual disabilities, but many of us have an average or above-average IQ. Please understand that autism is simply a different way of being, not an intellectual disability.

## Please Use the Symbol That Autistic People Prefer

When someone thinks of autism or wants to design a logo that everyone will immediately identify with autism, the puzzle piece is included because, years ago, it was selected as a representation of those who are autistic. Those who adhered to the medical model chose it, not the community. As far as the symbol itself goes, it did its job at the time. It was used to highlight autism in previous decades so that there would be some form of international symbol for autistic people. When something is relatively new to the public's awareness, like autism was back in the middle of the last century, raising awareness is an important thing.

However, while there are autistic people who still identify with the symbolism of the puzzle piece, most autistic people don't. The reason it is no longer widely accepted in the community is that the puzzle piece was created as a representation of people who suffer from a puzzling, complex condition, and that the symbol was disseminated without input from the autistic community. For us it has become a symbol of stigma. The reason it is a stigma to us is that it is a solitary jigsaw puzzle piece, which indicates we are a piece of a bigger puzzle where we don't have a place. For autistic people seeking support, guidance, and advice, or even to mix with other people, the puzzle piece on company and organizational logos often deters interaction with those groups. Despite most autistic people rejecting the puzzle piece, it remains in common usage today.

So, a new symbol was born: the gold infinity symbol. Originating through discussions at Autistic UK CIC, the gold infinity emblem was warmly welcomed by the community and became widely used and accepted in 2018. The infinity symbol has been adopted by neurodiversity advocates not only to show that the possibilities for us are endless, but because it is something we have chosen ourselves. The color gold is a great nod to autism because of the chemical symbol for gold, which happens to be Au (*Au*tism). For the broader neurodiversity crowd, the rainbow infinity symbol is used to be more inclusive of those who are not autistic but have other differences that make them the amazing and incredible souls that they are.

If only one school takes down their puzzle piece symbols and replaces them with the gold infinity symbol, this book will have been a huge success and a viable contribution to the autistic community by making the future brighter for the children growing up after us. A symbol that promotes inclusion, acceptance, and positivity, like the gold infinity symbol does, will only strengthen relationships and reduce the imposed shame many of us carry through life.

I identified with the puzzle piece at one stage, but now I don't. My preference is to respect and accept the symbol that most autistic people prefer. Some individuals may still prefer the puzzle piece, and that's fine as long as they are aware that most of us align with the gold infinity symbol that promotes positivity and no end to our potential.

## Please Don't View the Autistic Spectrum as a Scale of Severity

The concept of the spectrum itself is very misunderstood. The autistic spectrum is not a sliding scale of severity that goes from left to right or up and down. It is not a linear tool, as some people think, that ranks how *severely autistic* someone is. That is simply not the case. In some areas of the world, parents are told that their children are "stage 1" or "stage 2." This model of diagnosis only reinforces the incorrect way the autistic spectrum is viewed, almost like a "stage 2" is more "severe" than "stage 1" and, if you are not careful, your child will progress to "stage 3."

For certain privatized medical or therapy solutions, this can be a very sinister marketing tool. It almost implies that if parents do not select specific suggested therapies, their autistic child will somehow become "more autistic" and deteriorate. I am as autistic now as I was when I was born; the reason life became easier for me isn't because I was graded on a sliding scale of the spectrum that demanded certain therapies, but because I accepted myself. I never worsened or became "more autistic." We are not an illness that worsens over time.

The best way to view the autistic spectrum is by imagining it as a circle, not a line. On that circle there are many individuals, each with their own differences. We know that having more sensory needs doesn't make someone "more" autistic, and having more fine motor skills doesn't make someone "less" autistic. A color wheel is what you need to visualize! We are all different and unique, although in the autistic community, we may have similarities between us that make us our own diversity group. We have and represent differences. We do not have or represent disorders or diseases that progressively worsen. We are unique and individual; we are autistic.

## Please Do Not Use "Functioning" Labels

"Functioning" labels are used to determine the functioning levels of autistic people. Those like me who were diagnosed with Asperger's syndrome as a child might be labeled as having "high-functioning autism." From an outsider's point of view, I was "high functioning." I was always a high achiever academically, and I grew to establish a solid social work career. At the same time, I did have many disagreements with teachers because I did things differently. My methods may have been different, but they reached the same conclusion and sometimes the results were better, especially when I worked alone and not as part of a group.

As an adult, I achieved the things that I wanted to in life: I forged a good career, bought a house, wrote books, spoke at events, and established my own training platform. Combine all that and I often get labeled as "functioning at a high level." I sure wasn't too "high functioning" when I was waiting for my son to be born; the fear of the unknown crippled me emotionally. I was the proverbial basket case. I'm sure my parents and friends would agree: during that turbulent period of life I was anything but "high functioning."

The imagery of the phrase seems to indicate that someone is *less* or *more* autistic than someone else. I don't see myself as being more or less autistic than anyone else. It isn't a competition. The autistic spectrum is not a scale of severity or range. I believe the main reason many autistic people are not as functionally independent as I am is because they haven't been allowed to be independent. After so many years of feeling that everything they are doing is wrong, and going through hours of various therapies to be compliant with the rest of the world, the high- or low-functioning labels serve to instill lasting mental health conditions like depression and PTSD.

## Please Carefully Consider Compliance-Based Therapies before Using Them

Often when children are diagnosed as autistic, there is an immediate panic from parents who want to do everything they can to help and support their child. The word "therapy" has positive connotations, and it makes the parents' decision to send their child to compliance therapies much easier. The usual pathway is a referral for therapy after a child has been diagnosed. The ultimate goal of compliance therapy, whether therapists choose to admit it or not, is to make the autistic child indistinguishable from their peers.

There are therapists who dispute this, but autistic children ultimately do what their therapists want them to do instead of what they feel most comfortable doing. As a small child, if a therapist were to offer chocolate treats if I stopped walking around the classroom, I would have sat down and accepted the treats! I would have stayed in my seat until the next notion to walk entered my mind. The point is that this type of reward therapy gives a false impression that the "therapies" themselves are somehow working and that the children are happy to participate. The truth is that we are like anyone else; we like the reward, and most of us don't want to offend the therapist. The problems with rewards-based systems also hold true for activity- or play-based systems. Children will only learn to play in the mode that the therapist feels is most beneficial.

The consequences of compliance therapies can surface later in life and, as I've described in these pages, are often much more dire. The ingrained inability to self-advocate, to express and have a voice, lowers one's feelings of self-worth. You owe it to yourself and those around you to educate yourself about all aspects of therapies and how they may affect you later in life. Many autistic adults are speaking out about their experiences with such therapies; listen to those voices. To dismiss a large collective of voices only makes us forget the past when we need to learn from it.

It is the therapist that parents listen to when it comes to "progress." Ask if this is a means of suppressing autistic children. Ask who decides what is appropriate for the child. Ask if the child has a say in their play-based therapy and what they have to achieve to receive playtime. Ask the child how they feel when it is taken away from them. Then ask yourself how you would feel if someone took something special away from you to make you agree to sit still in class. Question, learn, and please communicate with your autistic child. Ask them how they feel about the therapies they are getting. Then listen to what the child is saying and why.

What if, instead of compliance therapies, we had acceptance and understanding training for teachers, parents, support groups, and employers? We realize the majority often decides what is normal and what is not normal, so I suggest we—the autistic community—work with the majority to make neurodiversity and acceptance the norm. There is always an onus on the children to partake in therapy and support, but what if we break the mold and ensure every teacher and parent has access to the right education when it comes to autism? Focus on the uniqueness, the abilities, the gifts, and the wonders that being autistic can demonstrate. I believe that autism is like a superpower, but it takes the correct level of nurturing for it to bloom. As my (possibly) fellow autistic Einstein once said, "All that is valuable in human society depends upon the opportunity for development accorded the individual."

## Please Don't Pin All Your Hopes (or Fears) on Diagnosis

A diagnosis, in and of itself, only serves one purpose: to tell people what they already know. This is usually true for adults who believe themselves to be autistic; they were correct, as well. If you aren't sure about the possibility that you or someone you love is autistic, seek a diagnosis, but if you know it, move toward learning more about it.

People believe that a diagnosis will give them a master key to the kingdom of support, knowledge, and assistance. It doesn't! Most people have to seek additional support and guidance on their own. I've found that a diagnosis mainly serves to have a medication review every so often, if medicines are even prescribed. Diagnosed or not, people join groups and voluntary services so that kids can meet similar kids and parents can gain hope from other parents. Of course, some have underlying learning disabilities and a diagnosis is required for the specialized aspects of disability. Here a diagnosis serves a very important purpose for those of us who may not be as independent as others. But even though a diagnosis is not always needed, it is, in every case, financially costly.

Many of those who identify as autistic don't need a diagnosis to tell them what they already know. Some might even feel hampered socially or financially by an official diagnosis because it might affect how others view them. Self-diagnosis is perfectly acceptable for those of us who don't want to or cannot afford to seek an official diagnosis. Allow me to be the first to welcome you with open arms.

## Please Consider Increasing Opportunities in the Workplace

As stated in chapter 10, "How Autistic People and Employers Develop Good Relationships," the employment rate for autistic people is tragically low. There are those of us who have multiple degrees, accolades, and academic awards, but even with those achievements, we are not given opportunities when it comes to employment. The recruitment system seems to be a problem for us, possibly because autistic people often falter at the interview stage. An employment interview seems to be a situation that not many of us can cope with. Imagine having an extreme level of qualifications but not being able to articulate them in an intimidating interview scenario. It is a problem that can be rectified; as I wrote, it requires communication on both sides.

It's a sad thought that some of the most talented individuals that mankind has to offer may be sitting at home, alone, because interviews are such a huge barrier for them. A more inclusive recruitment system could ensure that the best candidates always get jobs, not the people who can sell themselves and recite buzzwords best during the appointment. Currently autistic people have limited opportunities in the workforce. Of the individuals who are gainfully employed, job retention is also sometimes an issue. Part of the reason for that is because people's views on autism and of autistic people are so outdated that we aren't given a chance to shine.

A large portion of that is because autism awareness training may or may not be provided in the workplace. When it is provided, the people you are going to be working with are hearing about traits that stigmatize us further. These people are trying to learn about us; their intent is admirable, but it doesn't help when what is being taught presents the stereotypical depictions. Those include short attention span, impulsive repetitive movements, hyperactivity, being non-communicative, being nonresponsive, aggression, sensory issues, lacking emotion, and all the other disparaging descriptions. Imagine that someone wanted to learn about the indigenous tribes of the South Pacific. If you truly wanted to learn and understand the people, would you rather immerse yourself in the indigenous community itself or read perspectives from someone who has no firsthand knowledge of the tribe and has only viewed them from a distance? Those types of remote conclusions lead to assumptions that too often are not based on facts.

If neurodiversity were positioned as a basic protocol in global employment, the rate of employment for autistic people would improve from the meager figure it is now. Instead of unlimited money being invested in raising awareness of the things that bring us down, I suggest that the funds should be placed in neurodiversity training. Allow that money the ability to create happier and more confident children, comprehensive educational systems that support acceptance, and inclusive and efficient workplaces. That breeds better success. On a grand scale, this could literally improve the global economy, which could reflect favorably on health systems because we would be contributing more to the economy and tax base and relying less on public health systems.

We can work together to solve problems!

## Please, Stop Looking for Something to Blame

The other day, I saw a horrible post on social media about a large gathering of anti-vaccination protestors claiming that vaccines somehow made their children autistic. Of course, I will probably be called out for acknowledging that the original hypothesis has been universally rejected. Personally, I would much rather see these parents march for acceptance and understanding of their autistic child instead of searching for something to blame. I may be extreme here, but to me placing blame says, "I don't accept my child." Of course, they have the right to their beliefs, but I choose to follow science and to embrace the fact that I am autistic rather than looking for a place to lay blame. Something to note that is odd: I have never known an autistic person to attend anti-vaccine rallies and demonstrations. I wonder why that is. If even part of the research dollars that seek to find a "cause" were used to reboot information on autism, including neurodiversity acceptance and specialized training for educators and employers, I am 100 percent certain my community would thrive rather than hide in the shadows. It would help everyone be in a better state of mind.

If it were proven beyond all reasonable doubt that autism is caused by vaccines, I would accept it. I am a man of science, and if the global consensus proved that this now-debunked hypothesis was correct, I would be the loudest voice out there supporting the discontinuation! But that has not happened. And whatever the final determination of the cause of autism is, it shouldn't matter. People should be proud to be autistic. The fact that a person is autistic is never going to change; for them, acceptance is the only path forward. We are not only autistic; we are aware of who we are and know that acceptance would be helpful to the neurodiverse and neurotypical communities.

There are autistic children who are being told that vaccines, pollutants, and various other things are at fault for them not being like everyone else. Compound that with companies that capitalize on the fears of parents to sell their products. I saw a social media ad recently where a company that sold generic vitamins stated that their vitamins would "cure or reverse" autism "symptoms." These vitamins were not approved as a medical prescription and had the same basic ingredients as any other multivitamin supplements. This type of marketing is what keeps the global focus on autism's demeaning traits and a need to be "cured." When products like the vitamins are available in pharmacies or online stores, it only serves to drive us deeper into depression because they won't cure us, no matter how many we take. For some people who don't dig into what is behind the headline, it can raise hopes and then dash them because the product doesn't live up to its advertising. I suppose there will always be companies that attempt to take advantage of one group or another, so I suggest that you make it your personal challenge to research and verify anything before you try it.

## Embrace Neurodiversity

Every autistic child can be destined for great things, if only you allow them to be autistic.

I think it is time to shift the focus away from why autistic people are the way we are or how we can be "cured" and move to accepting us as individuals with differences. Neurodiversity is closely aligned to the autistic community, but it also encompasses things like ADHD, ADD, dyslexia, and more. Rather than labeling these things as "disorders," understand that they are different neurotypes that are outside of the norm. The symbol for neurodiversity is the rainbow infinity symbol, whose colors represent the collage of many neurotypes. The infinity symbol signifies the endless possibilities that await us when we, both neurotypical and neurodiverse, are unified and function together.

There has been criticism aimed at the neurodiversity movement. Some say that neurodiversity is only for those of us that are "high functioning." That simply isn't true. Like the symbolism of our rainbow infinity, neurodiversity embraces all because we recognize the differences that we have as individuals; we create a collective group. It is not about a sliding scale of judgment or fixing something that really isn't broken. There is no high or low degree of someone's place on the spectrum, just a celebration of differences!

## Autistic People *Need* to Live Longer Lives

The most shocking reality when it comes to autism is that, on average, our life expectancy is shorter than neurotypical people. Credible studies cited in chapter 11, "Why Are Autistic Lives So Short?," link autism and physical conditions such as epilepsy and gastric issues. Stress is also a major health issue, as it feeds numerous problems that manifest in the physical body. I feel a certain amount of stress when my routine changes or when an unexpected life event throws me a curveball, but I can't say it would feel the same for anyone else. For me stress has contributed to health issues that continue to surface as I edge closer to middle age. I was born with one kidney, I have an iron overload in my blood, my blood pressure is always slightly north of normal, and I'm prone to bouts of colitis. I don't know how long I am going to live; nobody does. But, according to health professionals, the stressors I felt as a child and teenager have accumulated and contributed to the deterioration of some of my preexisting health conditions.

I do *not* stand before you as a victim. I know that many of my stressful episodes were entirely my fault. It is neither healthy nor productive to assign blame to anyone, including and especially oneself. I had the choice to embrace and love my differences at a young age and I refused to do so. When I speak with groups of teenagers, I want to inspire and encourage them to accept themselves from a young age so that they don't have to experience the pain and disconnection I felt. I want to be the person my parents would have taken me to meet when I was a teen.

Fear promotes stress. I had the same fears as my parents when I was young: What would become of me in adulthood? Would I ever be able to live on my own? Could I function in the workplace? If, at a young age, I had been inspired to believe, to know, that I could achieve things because I had accepted myself, I would not have harbored so much fear for my future.

Our life expectancy can improve, and it will take work from everyone. If more embraced the fundamentals of neurodiversity, everyone would feel less stressed. Children would mature knowing that they are different and that it is okay for them to be different!

Health awareness needs to improve, and we need to learn how to release stress in productive ways. My creative release is communicating through the written word and dialogue with others, but I have autistic friends who are talented artists, singers, and dancers. There are others who find stress-release outlets in other productive ways, and I encourage them all. Sometimes we can't find words to adequately describe what we are feeling, especially when we are stressed. If we learn to channel that frustration into something that allows us to productively express and release what we are feeling, we can be a much healthier group.

A positive word means more to us than people realize. When we achieve something, we are no different than anyone else; we want to be appreciated and acknowledged for that accomplishment. What does that have to do with our life span? Actually, it has quite a bit to do with health, primarily mental health. Truthful acknowledgment lets us set our goals a little higher every time we accomplish something. It is not about living up to someone else's expectations; it's about reaching our own expectations. That promotes a good feeling about oneself. Appreciation of an accomplishment also lessens the stress we manufacture for ourselves. It's a trait all humans have; we have it to an extreme.

I think that when neurodiversity is better understood among the general population, we will naturally lessen the stressors we all place on ourselves. Acceptance can truly make a difference in alleviating stress.

## Autistic People Can Love and Be Loved in Return

One of the saddest things people associate with autism is the idea that we lack emotion and empathy. It is incredibly hurtful; it portrays that we are somehow robotic, or even subhuman! I am not an animated person; I don't often show what I am feeling, but please be assured, I do feel it. On a Sunday afternoon, Ethan and I were in the park. My son is a social butterfly and has a beaming Hollywood smile when we are photographed together. He's quite the opposite of his shy and awkward dad. Ethan wanted to join in a game, but the other children told him that he couldn't play. I knew exactly how he felt; I went through that when I was young. The difference between Ethan and I is that he got over it almost immediately and played alone. I was affected by the rejection and sadness more than he was and held on to that feeling for much longer!

Most autistic adults experienced exclusion as children, and we know exactly what it feels like. We may not show much on our faces or verbally respond, but that doesn't mean we don't feel the exact same pain as anyone else. We are not completely devoid of emotion and love, as some have described us. When I visit my parents, sister, or nephews I do not throw my arms around them and smile like a toothpaste model, but my love for them knows no bounds. There are times I can show extreme excitement; the thrill of seeing a book I have written on a bookshelf in a bookstore makes me uncharacteristically giddy!

We do have feelings. We are human, and we demonstrate our feelings in different ways. Please, allow us our personal ways of emoting, even when they don't show on the surface.

## If You Have the Chance to Be an Autistic Person's Hero— Take It!

If attitudes and perceptions about autism change, we will live longer and have more opportunities in the longer lives we live. Stay away from negativity of all types; it only reins in your true self, the one that wants to live life and grow and develop like neurotypical people. I know some autistic people need support more than others, but no matter how much support someone needs, we all have our gifts and talents that should be nurtured and encouraged in every way possible!

The notion that autistic people have "obsessive and repetitive" behaviors is all too common. Some leaders in various fields have either been confirmed as, or were almost certainly, on the spectrum. If Einstein's "obsession" with time and space weren't nurtured, we wouldn't know anything about the nature of reality. If Michelangelo's "obsession" for art were not nurtured, we wouldn't have the paintings on the ceiling of the Sistine Chapel in Rome. If every teacher in the world understood that all children have different neurotypes, no child would be left behind or unfairly labeled.

I dream of an education system that has neurodiversity at its core, where having a different way of thinking is valued and appreciated. I dream that someday there will be a global education system where teachers know the individual requirements of a student rather than treating the totality of the class as a communal experiment. Teachers would be even greater heroes. The focus on obtaining a certain ranking or set of results leaves children like us behind. If schools promoted the talents and passions of all pupils, a generation of happy and confident adults would follow. It's the same advice I give parents. Nurture your child's passions, no matter how trivial you believe they may be.

As parents and teachers of autistic children, you don't know who you have in your love and care. You could have a child who could change the world if their passions and interests are nurtured. You could have a future Nobel Prize winner. The possibilities are endless. Dulling the sparkle of autistic people may prevent something that could change mankind forever from coming to fruition. This doesn't just apply to children; this also applies to adults! When allowed to express themselves and work in the way best suited to them, the autistic adult currently working for you may come up with an idea that takes your company to a global level in a single bound. The autistic person who couldn't get through the job interview may be the person who could eventually cure cancer, if only they were given the opportunity to do so.

I hope that everyone, neurodiverse or neurotypical, can apply these principles to their daily lives. If everyone made a collective effort to embrace us, we would live longer, happier, and more productive lives. Allow us to use our voices; hear what we say and act upon our choices. Welcome people from the autistic community who want to further their education so that they have the knowledge to change the world, reform the laws, and help make this a better place for neurodiverse and neurotypical alike.

As a community, be proud of being autistic, find your talents and excel at them, expand your awareness of yourself and the world, and become the reason autism is embraced by all. We are intelligent, we are human, we are kind, we are talented, we are the future, and most important . . .

**_We are enlightened and we CAN change the world!_**

# Afterword:
# Loving Yourself Autistically
## by JayJay Mudridge

I don't know how I found my voice; I kept tepid and tiny for so long. Perhaps I was tired of being a lukewarm creature, performing the contorted, fawning facsimile they created when they molded my child-self to neuromajority standards. Or perhaps the tiredness broke and I realized it isn't all for naught if I can save others from not just the dredge and drudgery of ABA but the real harm it causes to autists.

Unmasking has been key, joyfully stimming with abandon. I am a soft light in the middle of sensory Hellfire, turning circles in place in the aisles of the grocery store with my hands a-flitter by my sides, rocking and tapping a beat on my knees. I see their eyes, pursed lips, and stares like stone, but I am Cronos and I consume their disapproval like a pill. In a world that wasn't made for you, loving yourself recklessly with abandon—loving yourself autistically—is the most rebellious thing you can do. And I am nothing if not a rebel.

# Acknowledgments

It is not often I struggle for words, although finding the words to describe my love and gratitude for everyone who has supported me throughout the writing of the book is nigh on impossible! Thank you to my parents, Eimear and Tony—who are both the main historians when it comes to the life of Jude Morrow—and my sister, Emily, my first true friend.

Ethan, my son and hero, has displayed fortitude and patience beyond his years when I have been sitting up late at night frantically typing my thoughts as they flowed through my restless mind. Although he is young, he has been my safety net. Not just for the writing of this book, but since he came into my life on the 23rd of July 2013.

When writing and compiling my manuscript, I had the eternal wisdom of both Devra Jacobs, as my agent, and Brit Elders. Without them, none of this would be possible. As an autistic person, I find that it can be hard for people to "get it." Thank you both for "getting it." To write my undying love and thanks to Michele Cohn, Richard Cohn, Brennah, Corinne, Chelsea, and the rest of the Beyond Words Publishing team would exceed the word count for the entire book!

Now for the biggest thank-you, to the proud autistic people and parents who have so bravely told their stories in this book. Telling a story and baring your soul is not easy, especially for many of us who have had difficult times in life due to not being accepted and embraced. I applaud and thank each and every one of you from the bottom of my heart. Your stories have inspired and moved me, like they will inspire and move everyone who reads them.

# Notes

## Preface

1. Robert B. Pippin, "Third Part," *Nietzsche: Thus Spoke Zarathustra, edited by Robert Pippin, translated by Adrian Del Caro, Cambridge Texts in the History of Philosophy* (Cambridge: Cambridge University Press, 2006), 19–88, doi:10.1017/CBO97805 11812095.007.

## Chapter 2: What Is Autism?

1. Leo Kanner, "Follow-Up Study of Eleven Autistic Children Originally Reported in 1943," *Focus on Autistic Behavior* 7, no. 5 (December 1992): 1–11, https://doi .org/10.1177/108835769200700501, previously published in *Journal of Autism and Childhood Schizophrenia* 1, no. 2 (1971): 119–45.

2. World Health Organization, "International Classification of Impairments, Disabilities, and Handicaps: A Manual of Classification Relating to the Consequences of Disease" (1980), 27, https://apps.who.int/iris/handle/10665/41003.

3. World Health Organization, "International Classification," 28.

## Chapter 8: Generally Accepted Therapies

4. "Dr. Ivar Lovaas," The Lovaas Center, accessed February 9, 2021, https://thelovaas center.com/about-us/dr-ivar-lovaas/.

5. Elizabeth DeVita-Raeburn, "The Controversy over Autism's Most Common Therapy," Spectrum, August 10, 2016, https://www.spectrumnews.org/features/deep-dive /controversy-autisms-common-therapy/.

6. Henny Kupferstein, "Evidence of Increased PTSD Symptoms in Autistics Exposed to Applied Behavior Analysis," *Advances in Autism* 4, no. 1 (2018): 19–29, https://doi .org/10.1108/AIA-08-2017-0016.

7. Svein Eikeseth, "Recent Critiques of the UCLA Young Autism Project," *Behavioral Interventions* 16, no. 4 (October 25, 2001): 249–64, https://doi.org/10.1002/bin.95.

## Chapter 10: How Autistic People and Employers Develop Good Relationships

8. The National Autistic Society, *The Autism Employment Gap: Too Much Information in the Workplace*, August 31, 2016, https://s3.chorus-mk.thirdlight.com/file /1573224908/63516243370/width=-1/height=-1/format=-1/fit=scale/t=444848 /e=never/k=59f99727/TMI%20Employment%20Report%2024pp%20WEB.pdf.

9. Lina Zeldovich, "Now Hiring: What Autistic People Need to Succeed in the Workplace," Spectrum, March 4, 2020, https://www.spectrumnews.org/features deep-dive/now-hiring-what-autistic-people-need-to-succeed-in-the-workplace/.

## Chapter 11: Why Are Autistic Lives So Short?

10. Tatja Hirvikoski, Ellenor Mittendorfer-Rutz, Marcus Boman, Henrik Larsson, Paul Lichtenstein, and Sven Bölte, "Premature Mortality in Autism Spectrum Disorder," *British Journal of Psychiatry* 208, no. 3 (2016): 232–8, https://doi.org /10.1192/bjp.bp.114.160192.

11. Michael A. Ellis, "Early Death in Those with Autism Spectrum Disorder," *Psychology Today*, October 7, 2018, https://www.psychologytoday.com/us/blog/caring-autism /201810/early-death-in-those-autism-spectrum-disorder.

12. Hirvikoski, "Premature Mortality."

13. Anne V. Kirby, Amanda V. Bakian, Yue Zhang, Deborah A. Bilder, Brooks R. Keeshin, and Hilary Coon, "A 20-Year Study of Suicide Death in a Statewide Autism Population," *Autism Research* 12, no. 4 (January 21, 2019): 658–66, https://doi .org/10.1002/aur.2076.

14. Michael A. Ellis, "The Link between Suicide and Autism," *Psychology Today*, February 10, 2019, https://www.psychologytoday.com/us/blog/caring-autism /201902/the-link-between-suicide-and-autism; Sami Richa, Mario Fahed, Elias Khoury, and Brian Mishara, "Suicide in Autism Spectrum Disorders," *Archives of Suicide Research* 18, no. 4 (April 8, 2014): 327–39, https://doi.org/10.1080/1381 1118.2013.824834.

15. Hannah Furfaro, "Autistic Women Twice as Likely as Autistic Men to Attempt Suicide," Spectrum, August 7, 2019, https://www.spectrumnews.org/news/autistic -women-twice-as-likely-as-autistic-men-to-attempt-suicide/.

16. University of Utah Health, "Suicide Risk in People with Autism," ScienceDaily, January 23, 2019, www.sciencedaily.com/releases/2019/01/190123082225.htm.

17. Apoorva Mandavilli, "The Lost Girls," Spectrum, October 19, 2015, https://www .spectrumnews.org/features/deep-dive/the-lost-girls/.

18. Joseph Guan, Ashley Blanchard, Carolyn DiGuiseppi, Stanford Chihuri, and Guohua Li, "Homicide Incidents Involving Children with Autism Spectrum Disorder as Victims Reported in US News Media, 2000–2019," preprint, submitted June 23, 2020, https://doi.org/10.21203/rs.3.rs-37341/v1.

19. Mark T. Palermo, "Preventing Filicide in Families with Autistic Children," *International Journal of Offender Therapy and Comparative Criminology* 47, no. 1 (February 1, 2003): https://www.researchgate.net/publication/10877780 _Preventing_Filicide_in_Families_With_Autistic_Children.

20. Michael Zennie and Snejana Farberov, "'Alex Will Not Suffer under the System': How Mother Killed Her Autistic Teenage Son after He Was Restrained in a Hospital Bed for 12 DAYS by Doctors Who Couldn't Understand He Had a Serious Stomach Illness," *Daily Mail*, last modified August 31, 2013, https://www.dailymail.co.uk /news/article-2407771/How-Dorothy-Spourdalakis-killed-autistic-teenage-son -Alex-restrained-hospital-bed-12-DAYS-doctors-understand-stomach-illness.html.

21. Emily Willingham, "If a Parent Murders an Autistic Child, Who Is to Blame?," *Forbes*, September 5, 2013, https://www.forbes.com/sites/emilywillingham/2013/09/05/if-a-parent-murders-an-autistic-child-who-is-to-blame/.

22. Susan Hatters Friedman and Phillip J. Resnick, "Child Murder by Mothers: Patterns and Prevention," *World Psychiatry* 6, no. 3 (October 2007), 137–41.

23. Crystal Bonvillain, "Video Shows Florida Mom's 1st Attempt to Drown 9-Year-Old Son with Autism," Fox News, May 27, 2020, https://www.fox23.com/news/trending/watch-video-shows-florida-moms-1st-attempt-drown-9-year-old-later-found-dead/ZVKLLWPUI5G33CYSNKDVZRFKU4/.

24. NBC News, "Desperate Act: Mom Accused of Trying to Kill Autistic Daughter," September 2, 2014, https://www.nbcnews.com/health/health-news/desperate-act-mom-accused-trying-kill-autistic-daughter-n155816.

25. Eilidh Cage and Zoe Troxell-Whitman, "Understanding the Reasons, Contexts and Costs of Camouflaging for Autistic Adults," *Journal of Autism and Developmental Disorders* 49 (2019): 1899–1911, https://doi.org/10.1007/s10803-018-03878-x.

26. Virginia Chaidez, Robin L. Hansen, and Irva Hertz-Picciotto, "Gastrointestinal Problems in Children with Autism, Developmental Delays or Typical Development," *Journal of Autism and Developmental Disorders* 44 (2014): 1117–27, https://doi.org/10.1007/s10803-013-1973-x.

27. Alex Hamilton, "Stress Is a Leading Cause of Premature Deaths," The American Institute of Stress, October 2, 2019, https://www.stress.org/stress-is-a-leading-cause-of-premature-deaths.

28. Roberto Canitano, "Epilepsy in Autism Spectrum Disorders," *European Child & Adolescent Psychiatry* 16 (2007): 61–66, https://doi.org/10.1007/s00787-006-0563-2.